DesignOriginals

NOTEBOOK DOODLES

Peace Love AND MUSIC

JeSS ♥ VOLiNSKi

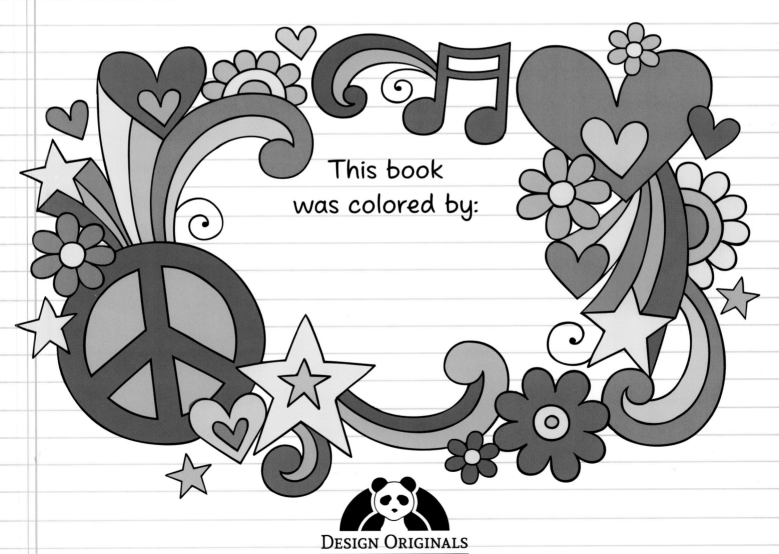

This book
was colored by:

DESIGN ORIGINALS
an Imprint of Fox Chapel Publishing
www.d-originals.com

Be YOURSELF to be creative

The thing I love most about art—making it myself or enjoying others' creations—is that **art allows you to be yourself by expressing yourself.** Whatever you love, whatever is important to you, whatever makes you who you are should come out in your art. By making art that matters to you, you're starting a conversation with everyone who sees it. You're saying, "Hey! This matters to me. What do **you** think about it?"

You might be wondering, how exactly do I express myself with art? That's where **The Elements of Art** come in. You might remember these from art class. Just like writers use words to tell a story, artists use these visual elements to express themselves and start their art conversation. All visual art—whether it is a painting in a museum, storyboards for a movie, a pattern on a bag, or a coloring book page—uses some combination of these seven basic building blocks of art. Not all art has to include all seven elements, but most art will include a few.

The Elements of Art

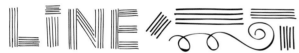

A **line** is formed as the connected distance between two points. Lines can be thick or thin, straight or curved.

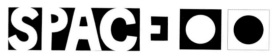

Space refers to the areas in a piece of art that are around or within different parts of the art. There are two kinds of space: negative (space around areas), and positive (space within areas).

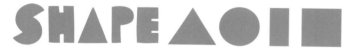

A **shape** is a defined area of space—a circle, square, blob, or a flower petal are all shapes.

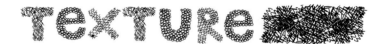

Texture refers to the way the art physically feels when touched, or how an artist visually makes the art **look** like it would feel. Shading with pencils is an example of this type of visual texture.

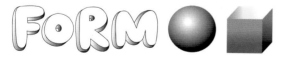

Something has **form** if it has volume (or creates the illusion of volume). A three-dimensional sculpture has form. A two-dimensional drawing with shading that makes it appear three-dimensional can also have form.

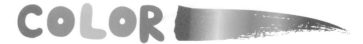

Color is created when light hits an object and is reflected to our eyes. A color can be described with three properties: hue (the color's name, such as "red"), value (how light or dark the color is, also called a tint or shade of the color), and intensity (how vivid or dull the color is).

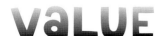

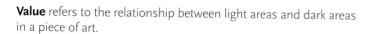

Value refers to the relationship between light areas and dark areas in a piece of art.

The Elements of Art IN ACTION

Let's look at one of my doodles and see what Elements of Art are here. Even though this is just a simple black and white drawing, it has line, shape, and space. When you color it in, you'll probably add form, color, value, and maybe even texture. That's all seven Elements of Art—on a coloring book page! How cool is that?! Art truly is all around us!

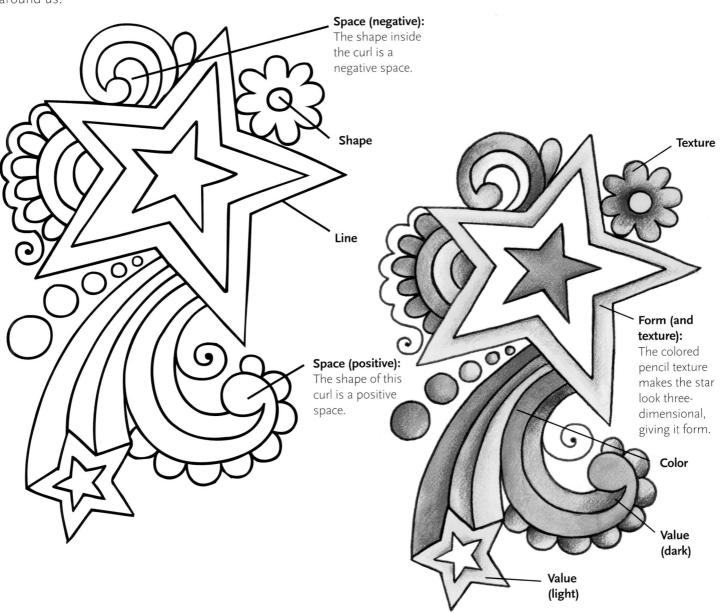

Space (negative): The shape inside the curl is a negative space.

Shape

Line

Space (positive): The shape of this curl is a positive space.

Texture

Form (and texture): The colored pencil texture makes the star look three-dimensional, giving it form.

Color

Value (dark)

Value (light)

Get inspired by COLOR

When it comes to expressing emotion, I think color is probably the most powerful Element of Art. To me, there's no better way to express how you're feeling, or how you want someone else to feel, than through the use of color. Just think of some of your favorite memories and how they make you feel. I bet color plays a big part of what you remember. Whether it's a beautiful sunset, the green of spring after a long, cold winter, or a perfectly clean, white expanse of snow, color makes a huge impact on us, both visually and emotionally. Just look at the way different colors can give the same flower drawing a completely different feel.

I've found that planning is key when working with color. If you're like me and you just **love** color, it might seem a bit overwhelming to get started. There are just so many color choices! And it's easy to fall into the rut of using the same colors over and over again, just because you like them. Making color decisions before you start can make you feel comfortable using new colors. Plus, you won't have to make a choice when you're in the midst of coloring and decide you don't like the result as much as you thought you would. A great way to try some new color combinations is to take a few minutes—it won't take long!—to create your own palettes before you get started.

Here's a fun trick I've learned for making palettes. It works especially well if you're using markers or colored pencils. Lay out all of your markers (or pencils) on a table or floor so you can see every single color you have. Pick one favorite marker (pencil) that will serve as the **anchor color** for your palette. Make it a color you really enjoy working with (or for a challenge, maybe a color you never work with). Now, pick two or three other markers (pencils) that complement your anchor color and place those next to your anchor color to start building a palette. Keep going until you have picked five or six colors. At this point, you don't even have to use them—you're just putting them side-by-side to see how the colors look together. Keep adding or switching colors until you like what you see. It's so easy to swap different colors in and out this way. Once you have a group of colors that you like, test them out on paper to make sure you still like the way they look together. If you love it, be sure to create a sample page with the names of the markers/colors you used so you won't forget. This is a great way to quickly create a whole library of color palettes for yourself.

Another great place to get color inspiration is literally from the world around you. Color is everywhere—your clothing, your bag, even a tissue box—there are probably patterns and designs with interesting color palettes surrounding you now! I'm sure there are things you bought because you liked the colors, so use those things that you love as inspiration. I once bought a pack of hair elastics simply because they had the most beautiful combination of blues and purples. Almost anything, anywhere, can become a color inspiration, so always keep your eyes open!

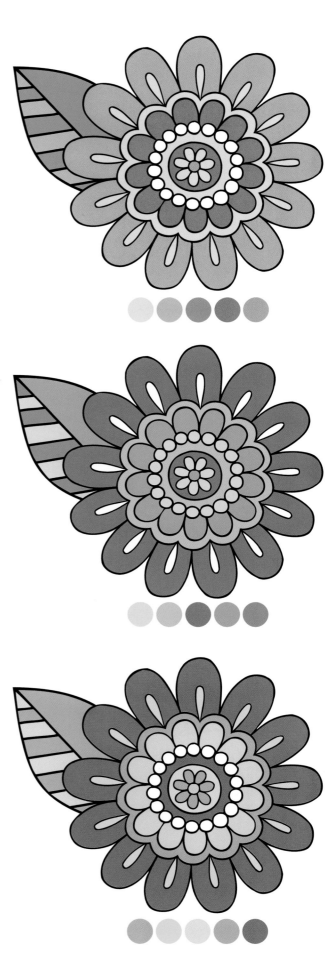

A SPECTRUM of Emotion

Color can be a great way to express yourself and define your mood. When you sit down to color, ask yourself, "How do I feel today? How can I use color to express that feeling?" Sometimes you might even feel something you can't quite put into words, but you can express it with color.

I've included some of my favorite palettes on the following page. Each one is paired with the emotion that best describes how the color combination makes me feel. But keep in mind that everyone is different, and that's what makes art so exciting. I love to use bright colors, but maybe you like more subdued colors. My "relaxed" palette might be your "cozy." There is no right or wrong when it comes to color! Use these palettes as a starting point and see how they make you feel. Try adding or taking away a color to customize the palette to reflect your taste and style. Then, make your own page full of YOUR favorite color palettes!

The next few pages contain some colored examples. You'll see two color palettes on each page, one at the bottom and one along the outer edge. The palette at the bottom shows the design's main colors in the large circles. The small circles show lighter colors (called tints) and darker colors (called shades) of those main colors. This is to give you the feeling of this palette and visually show which colors are dominant in the design (the bigger the circle, the more dominant the color).

Along the outer edge of each page, I've included a palette with each individual color, shown separately, so you can easily match your marker, pencil, or paint colors to the colors I used.

Whether you use one of my palettes or create your own, always be sure the colors you choose reflect who you are and how you're feeling.

Now go gather up your art supplies—it's time to color!

The circles along the outer edge of the gallery pieces show you each individual color I used in that particular piece. If you like the palette I chose, you can use these circles to match the colors of your own pencils or markers.

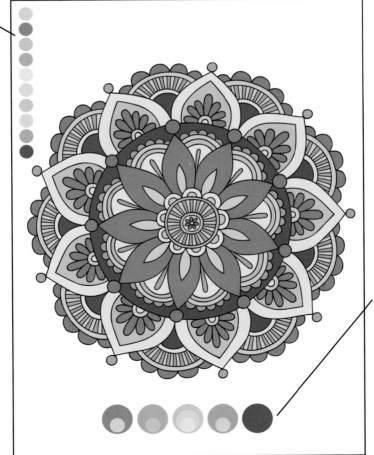

The circles along the bottom of the gallery pieces show you which colors are more dominant in each design. The larger the circle, the more dominant the color. The smaller circles show tints and shades of a main color that were introduced for variety.

A SPECTRUM of Emotion

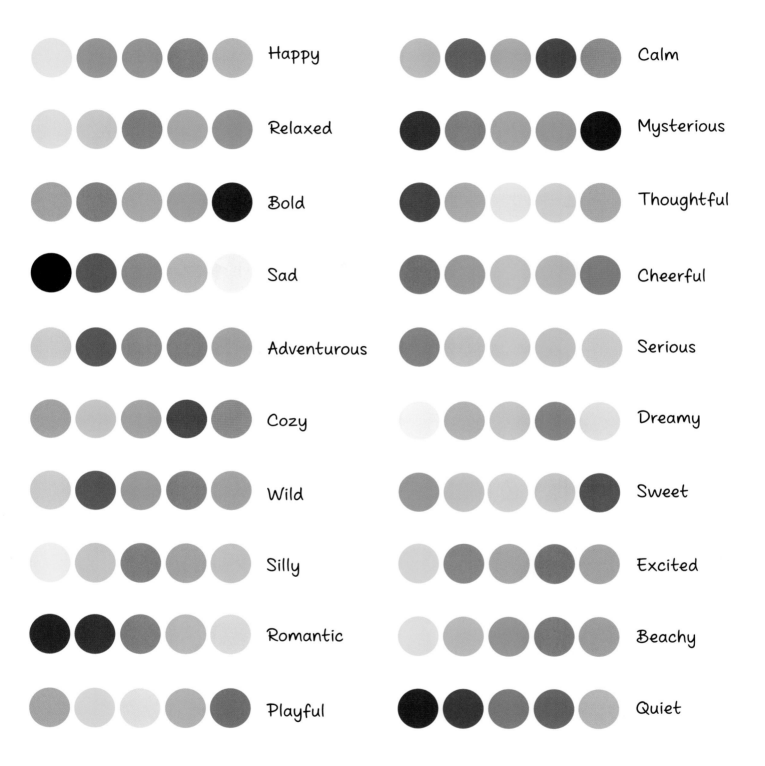

Happy

Relaxed

Bold

Sad

Adventurous

Cozy

Wild

Silly

Romantic

Playful

Calm

Mysterious

Thoughtful

Cheerful

Serious

Dreamy

Sweet

Excited

Beachy

Quiet

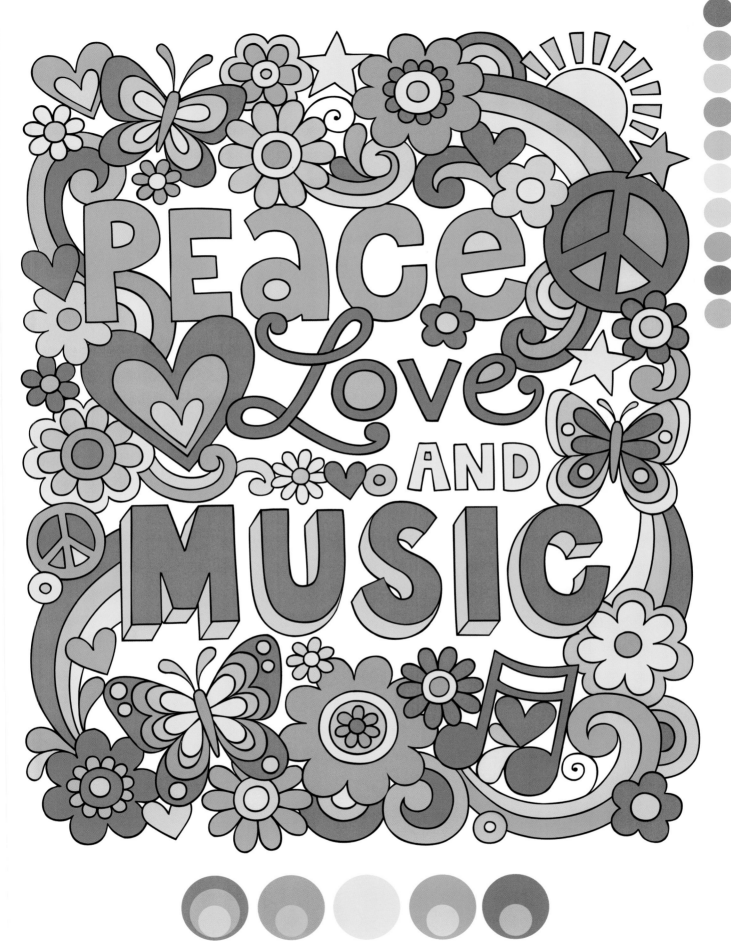

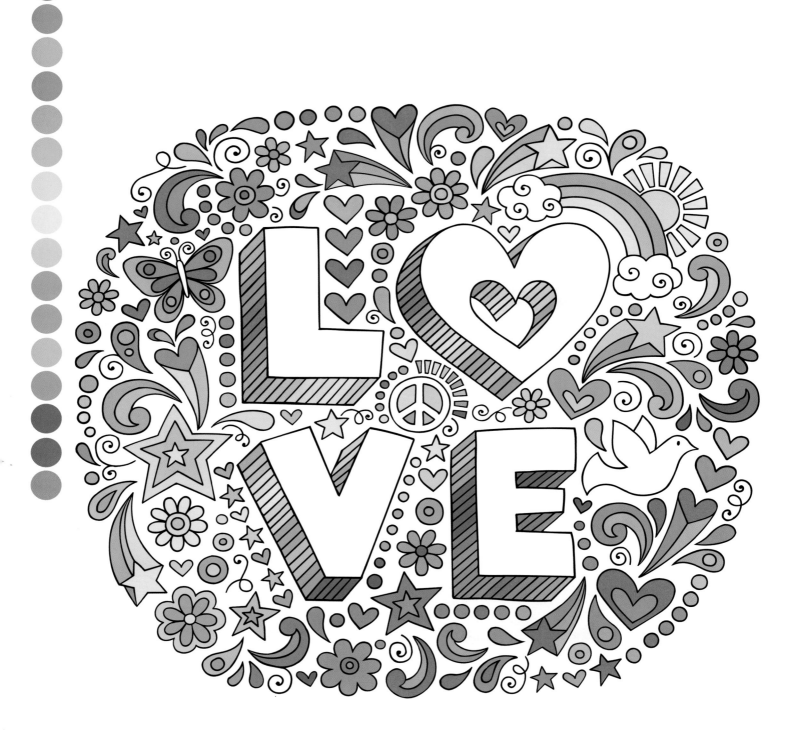

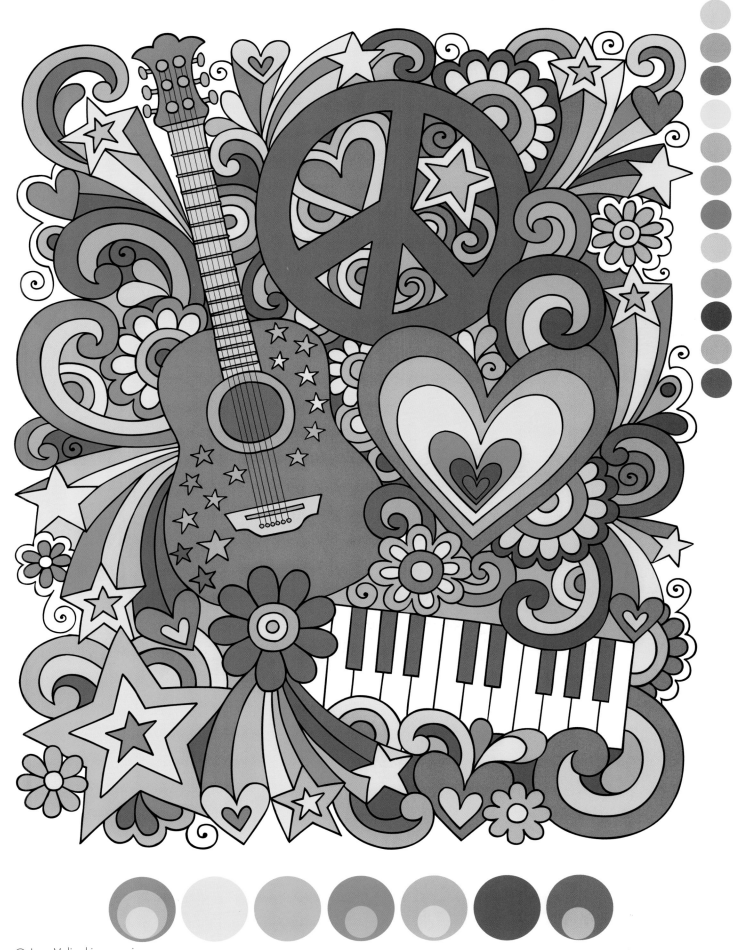

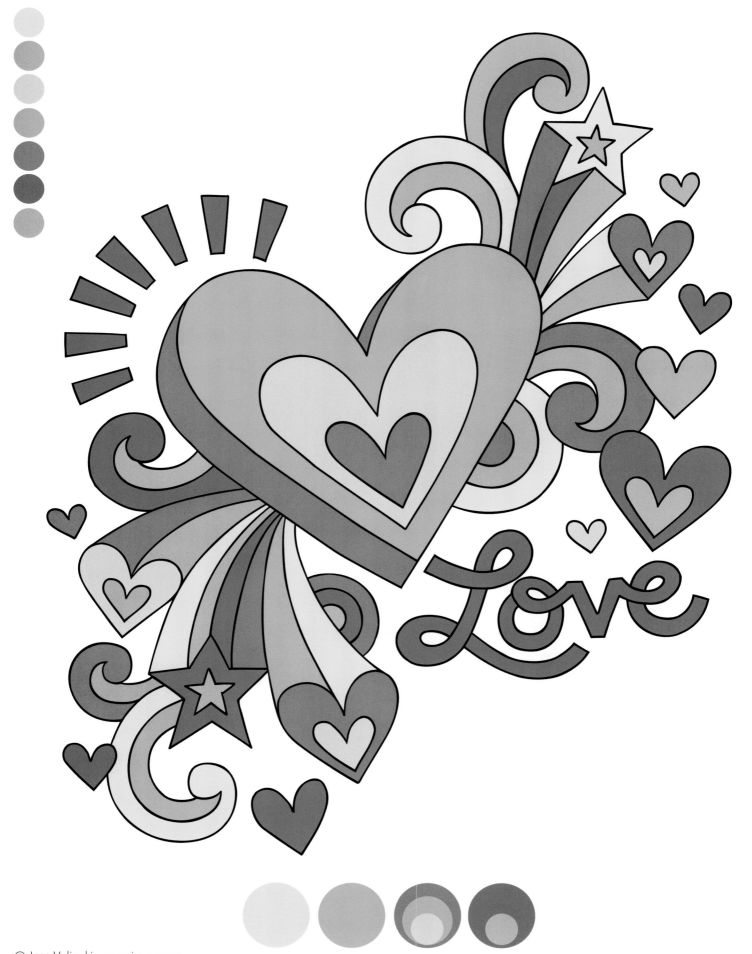

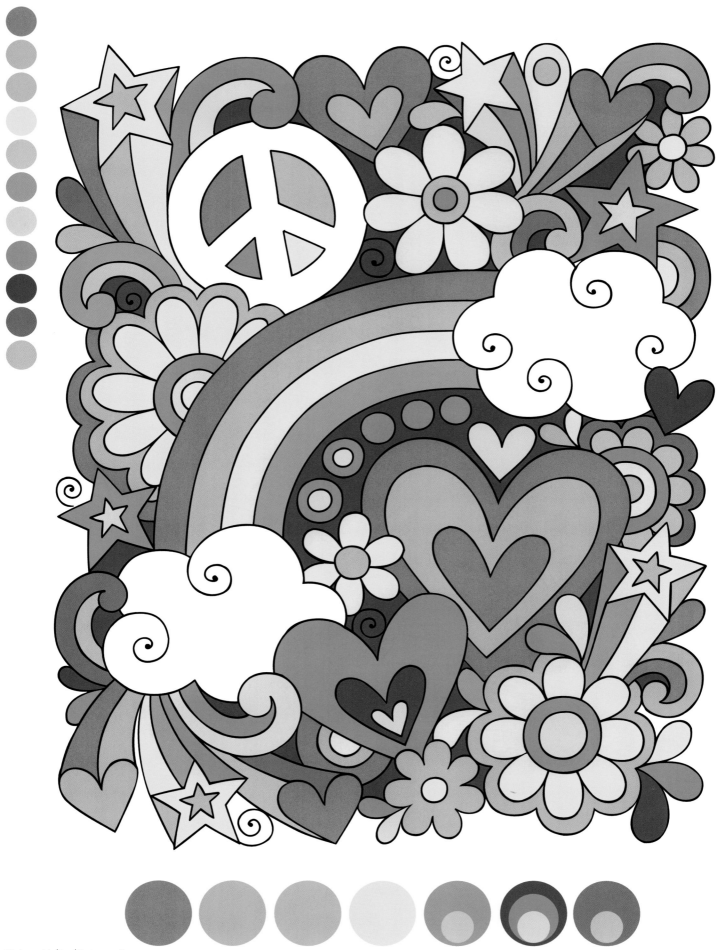

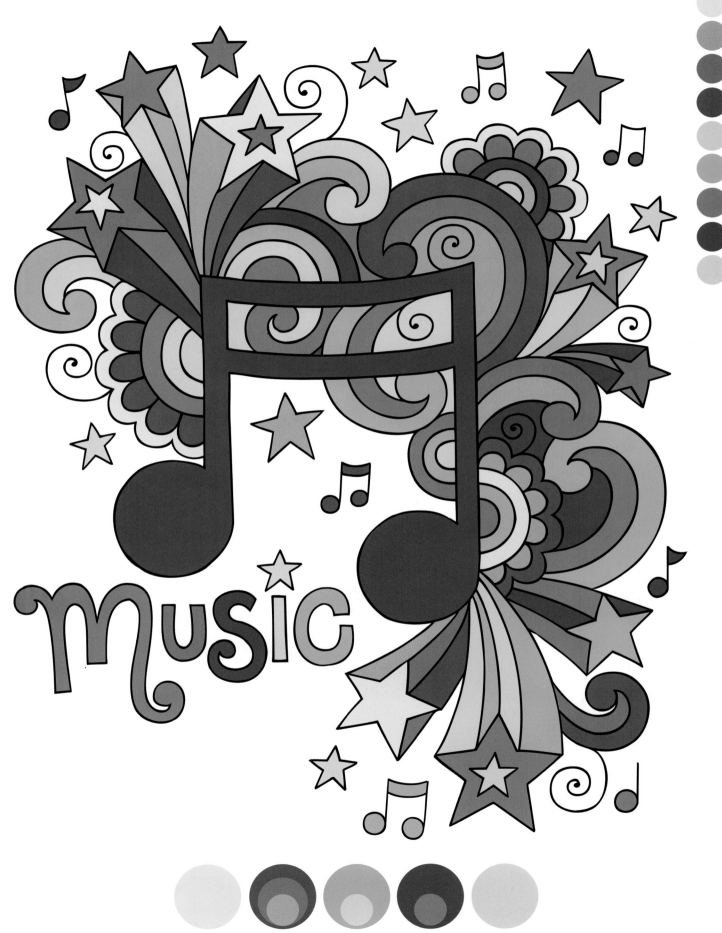

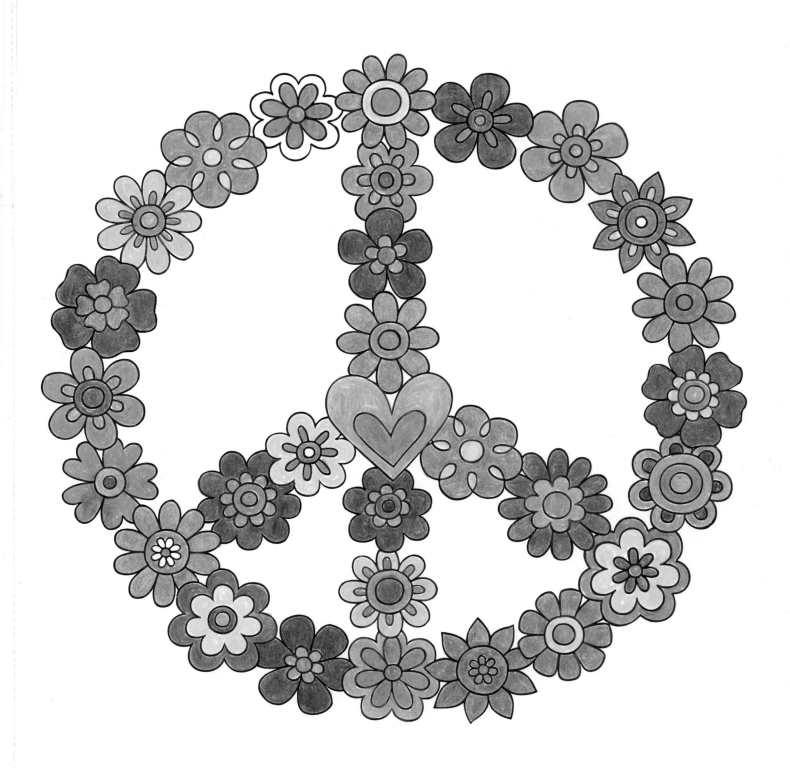

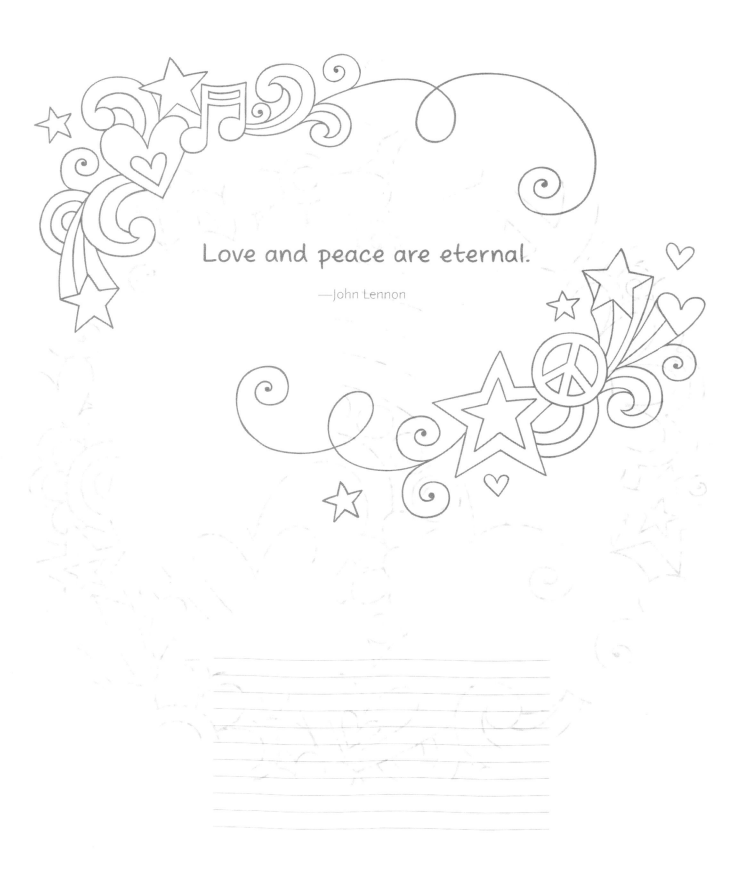

Love and peace are eternal.

—John Lennon

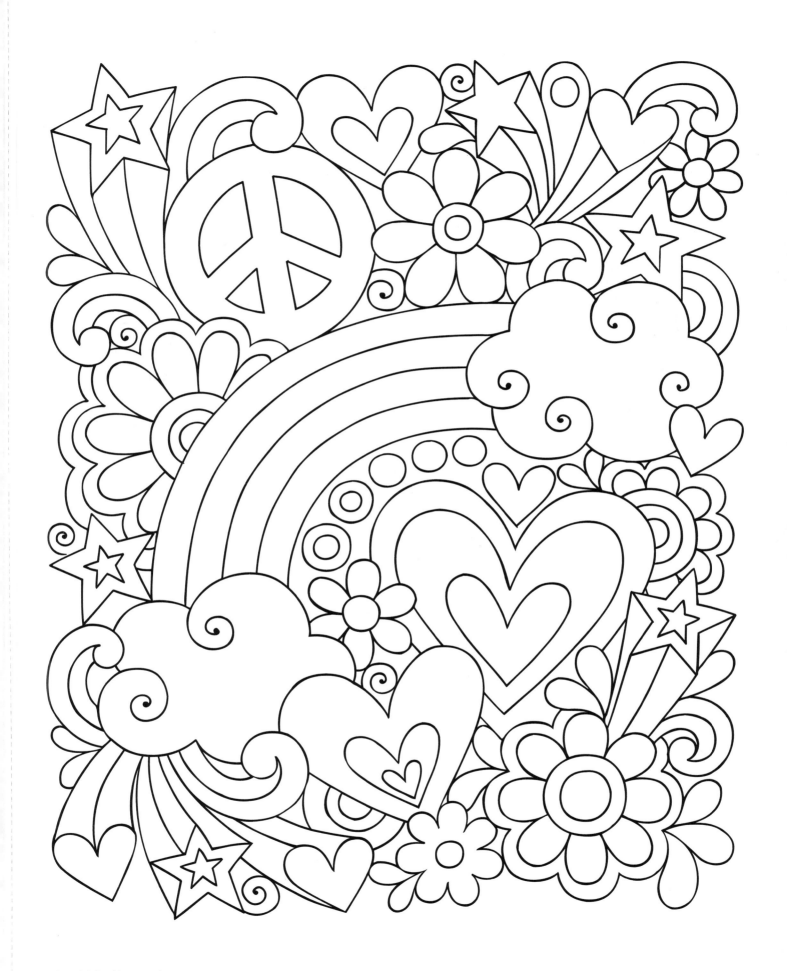

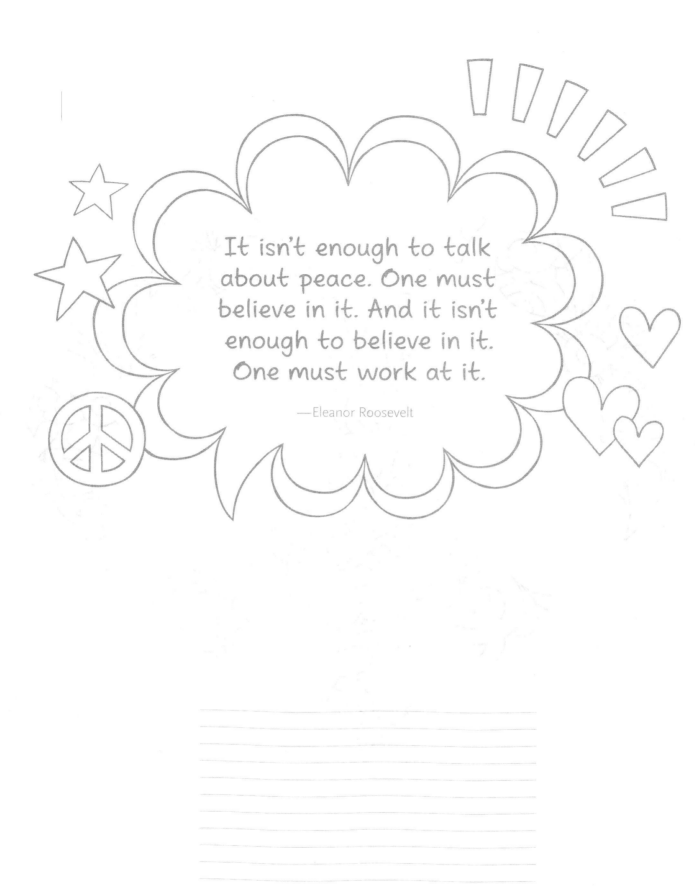

It isn't enough to talk about peace. One must believe in it. And it isn't enough to believe in it. One must work at it.

—Eleanor Roosevelt

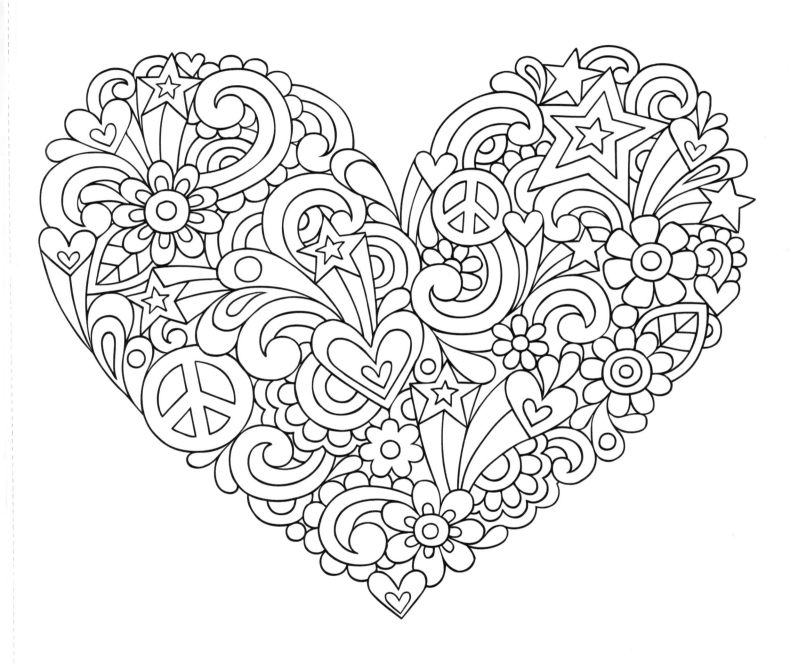

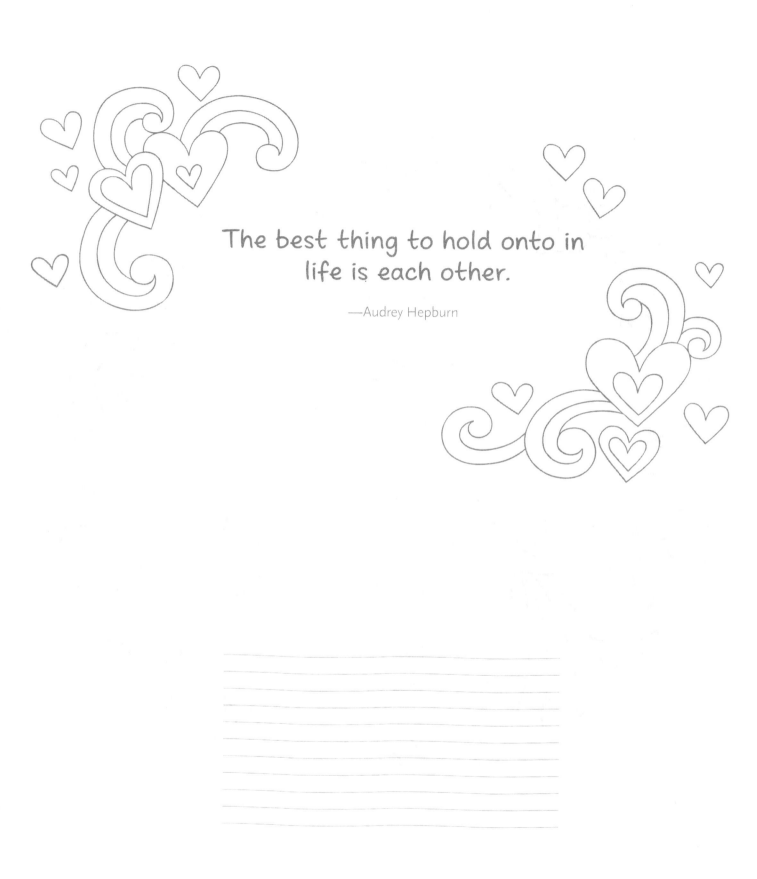

The best thing to hold onto in
life is each other.

—Audrey Hepburn

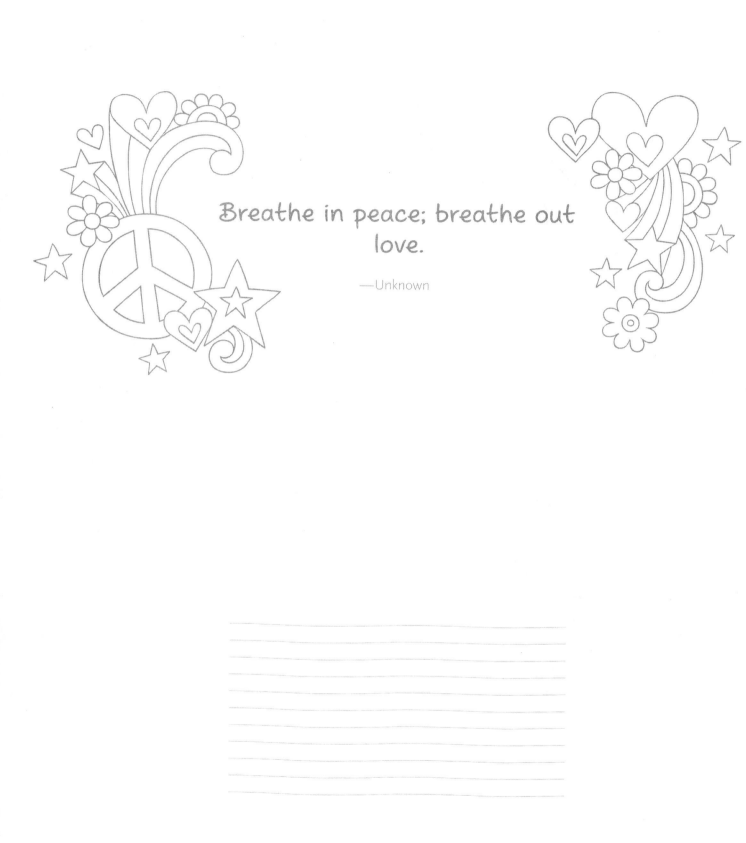

Breathe in peace; breathe out love.

—Unknown

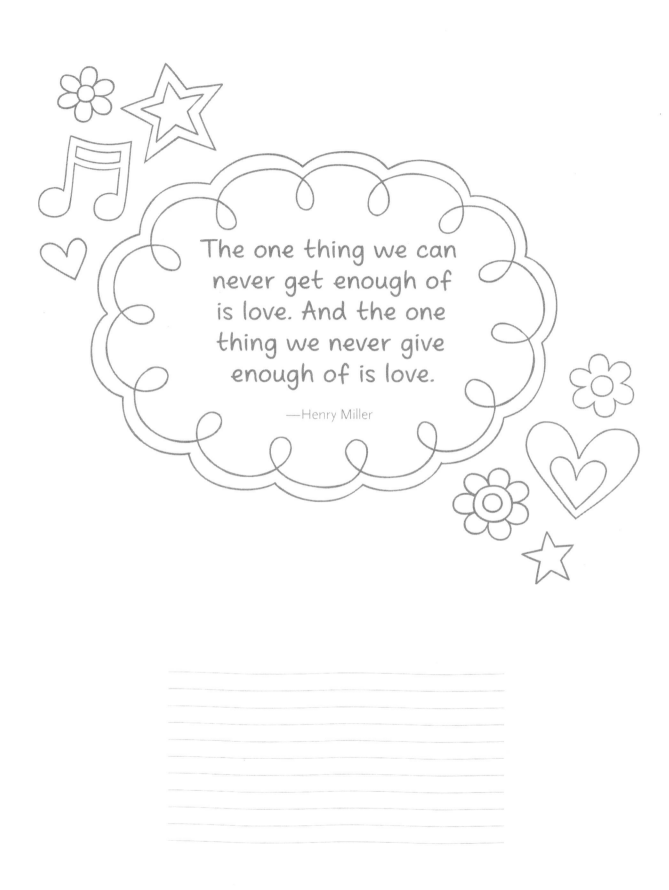

The one thing we can never get enough of is love. And the one thing we never give enough of is love.

—Henry Miller

Now it's your turn! Decorate each heart with a unique doodley pattern.

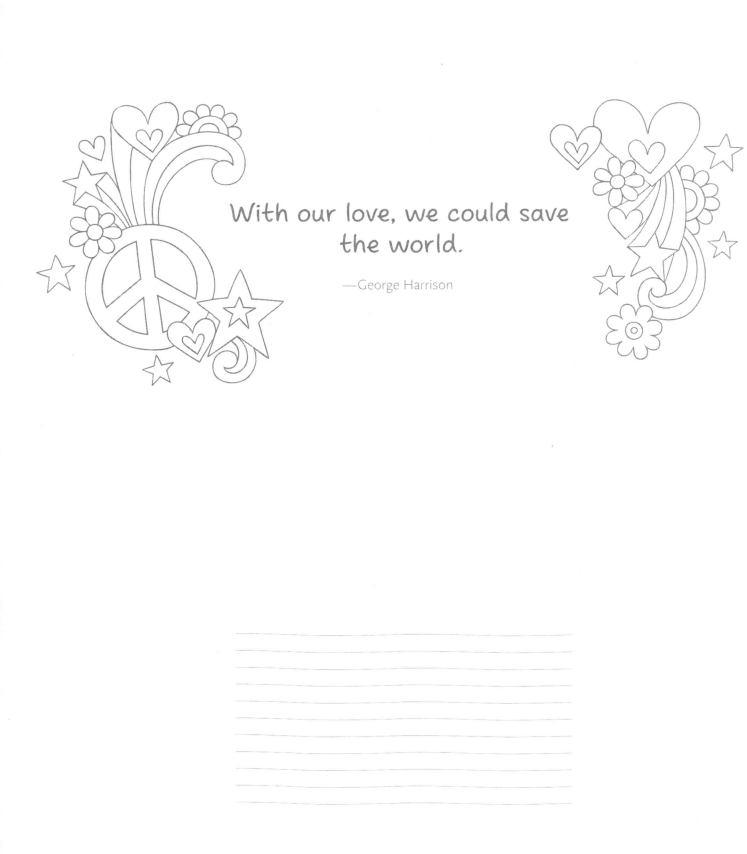

With our love, we could save
the world.

—George Harrison

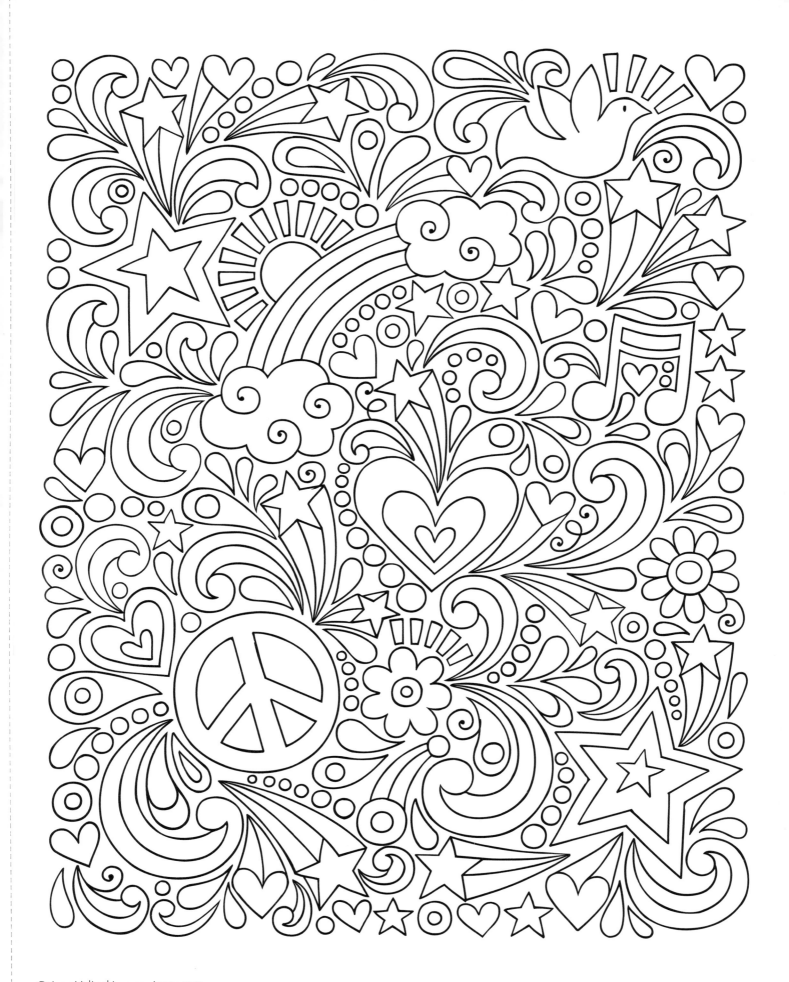

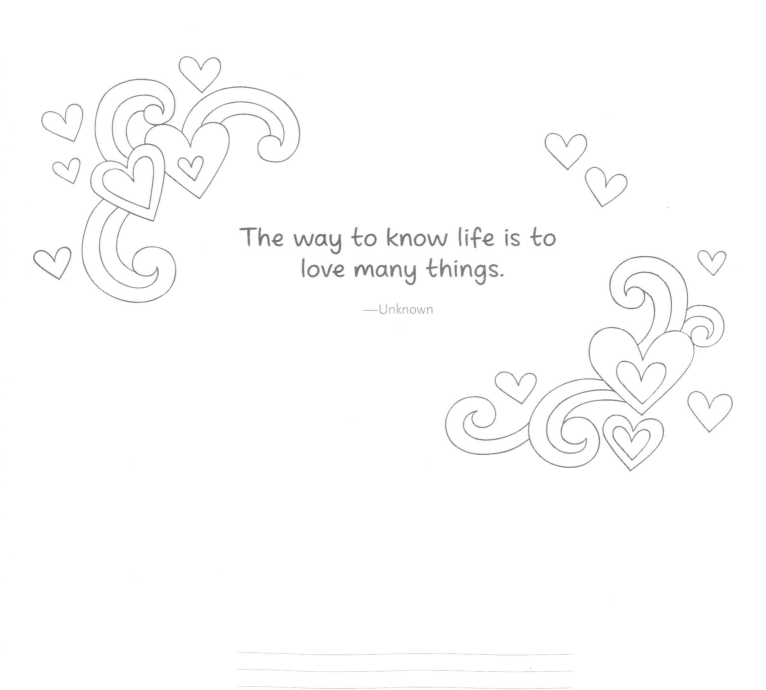

The way to know life is to love many things.

—Unknown

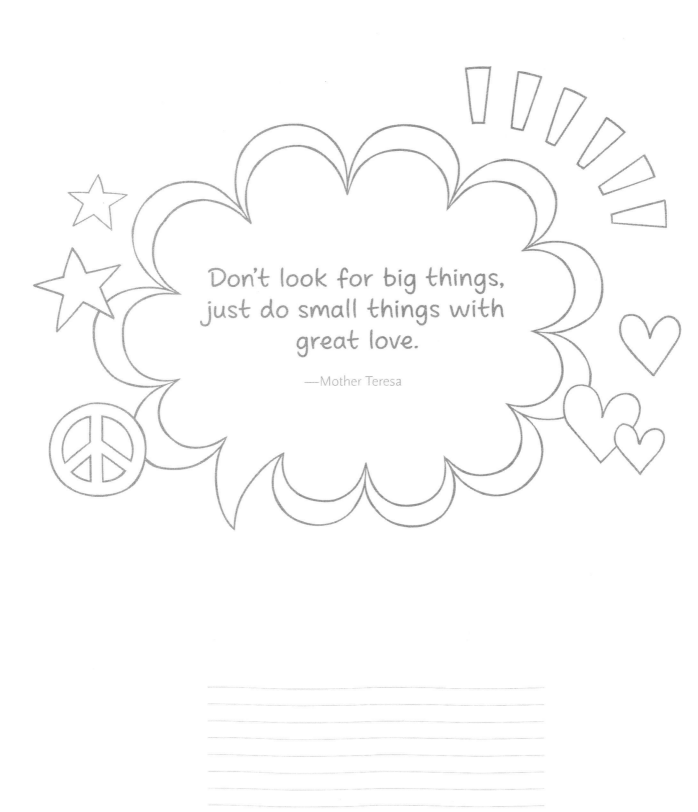

Don't look for big things,
just do small things with
great love.

—Mother Teresa

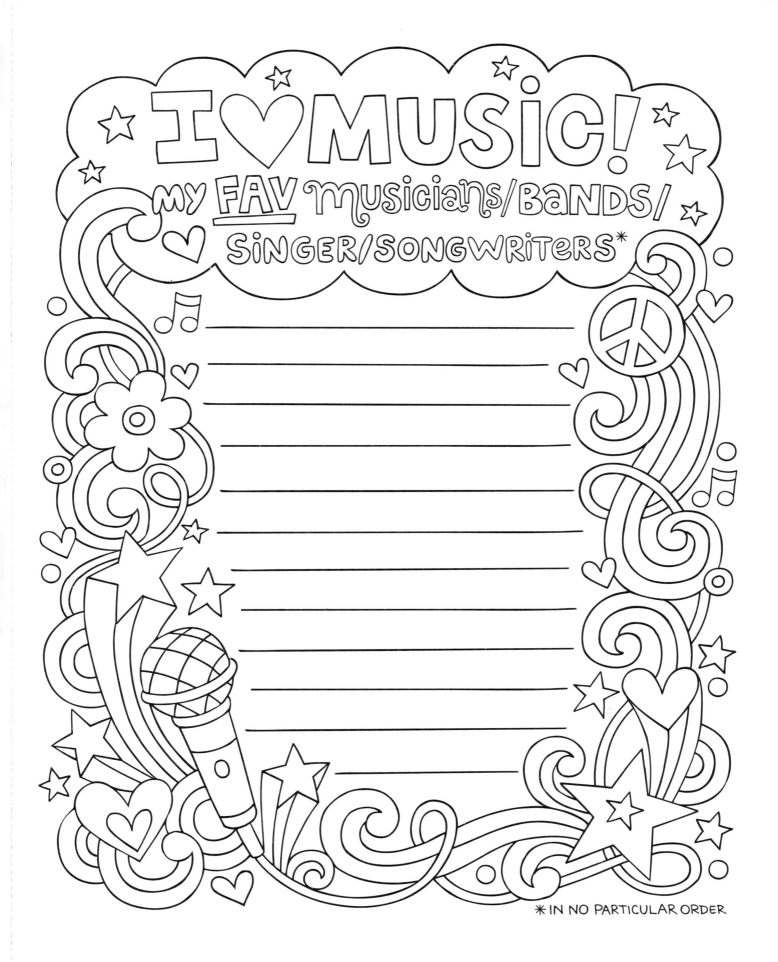

I ♥ MUSIC!
MY FAV musicians/BANDS/
SINGER/SONGWRITERS*

* IN NO PARTICULAR ORDER

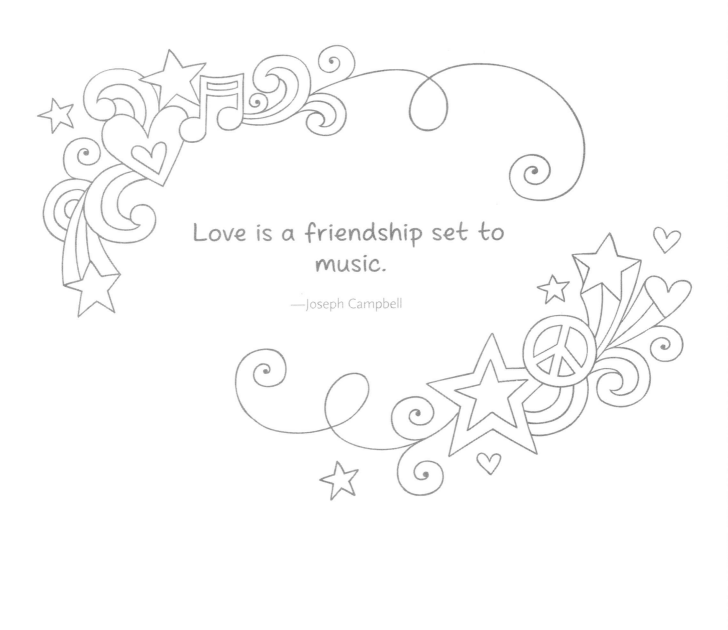

Love is a friendship set to music.

—Joseph Campbell

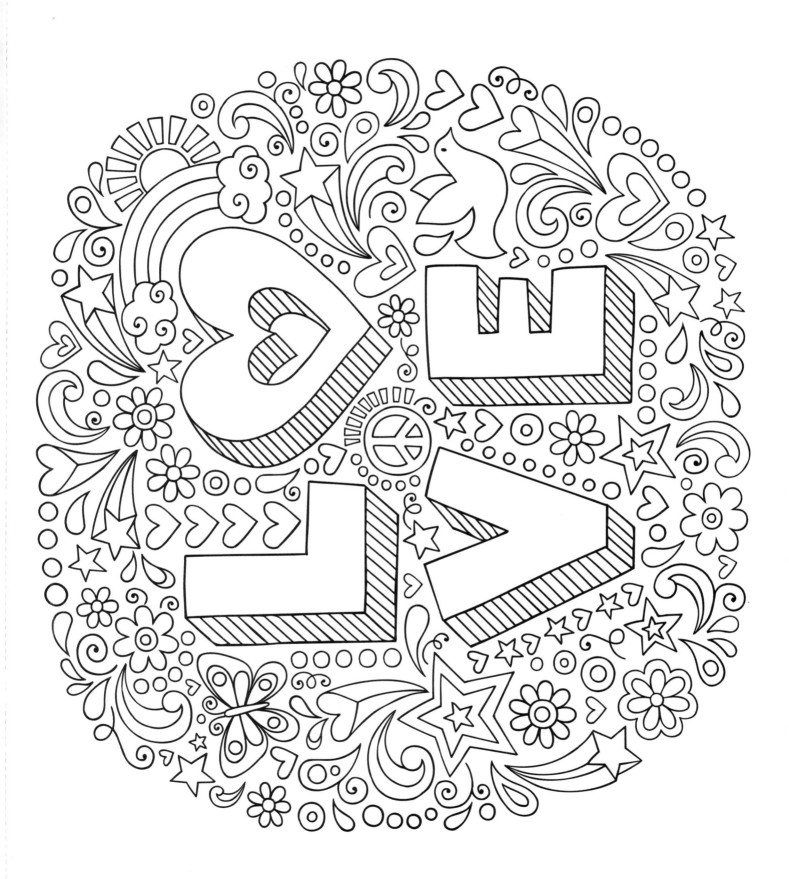

Work like you don't need
the money. Love like you've
never been hurt. Dance like
nobody's watching.

—Satchel Paige

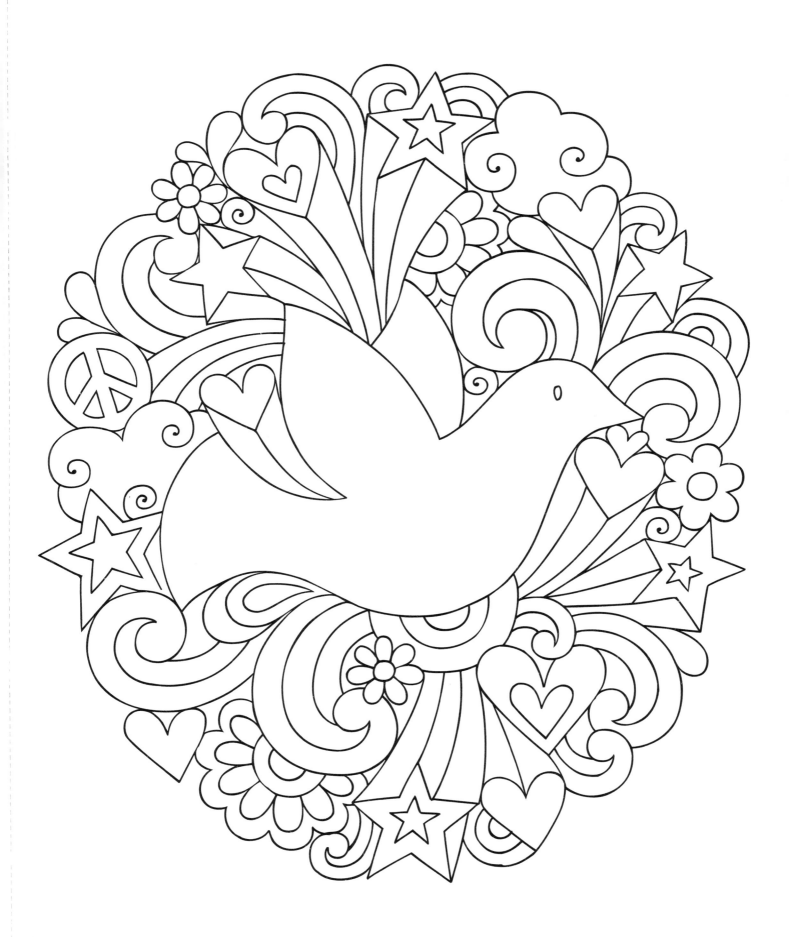

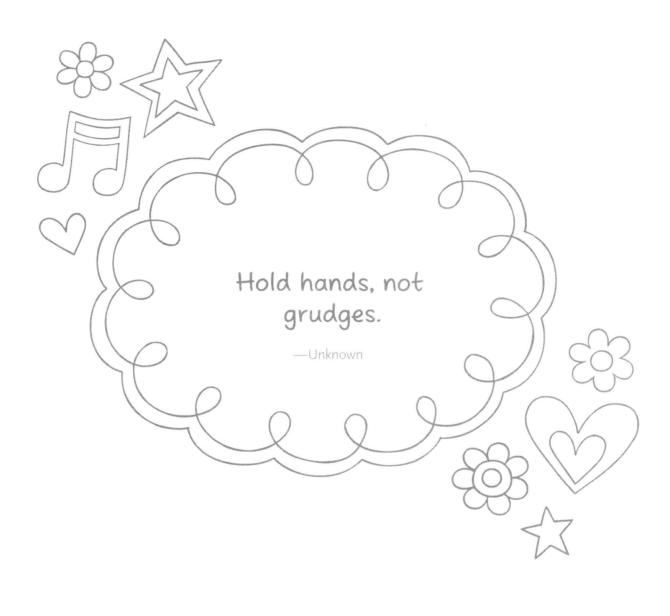

Hold hands, not grudges.

—Unknown

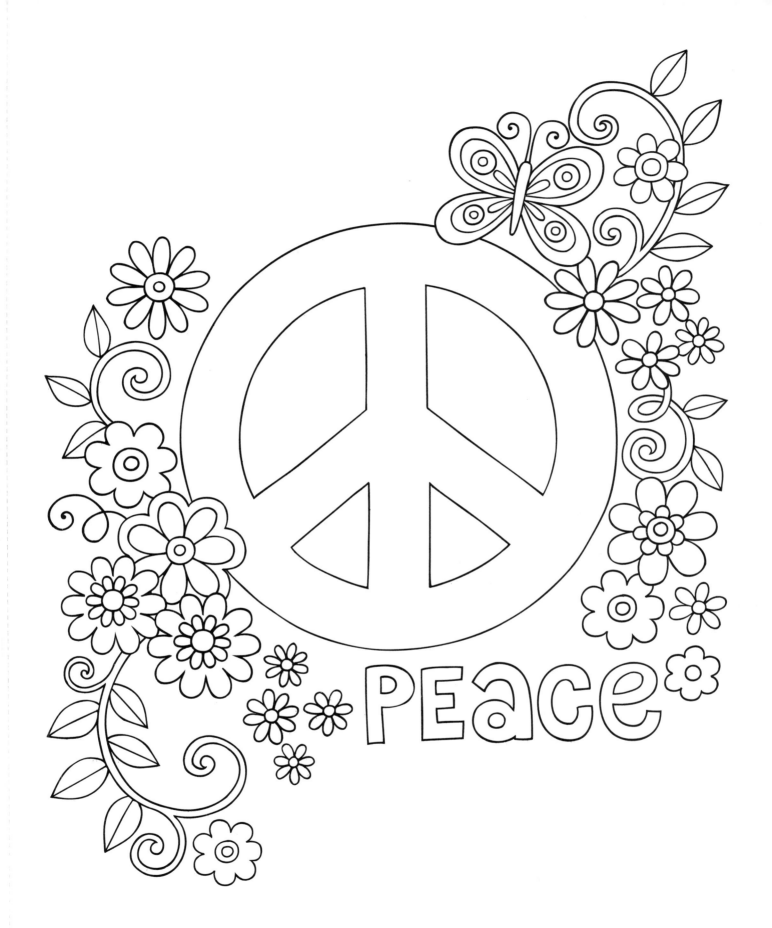

Decorate the peace sign with lots of colorful doodles!

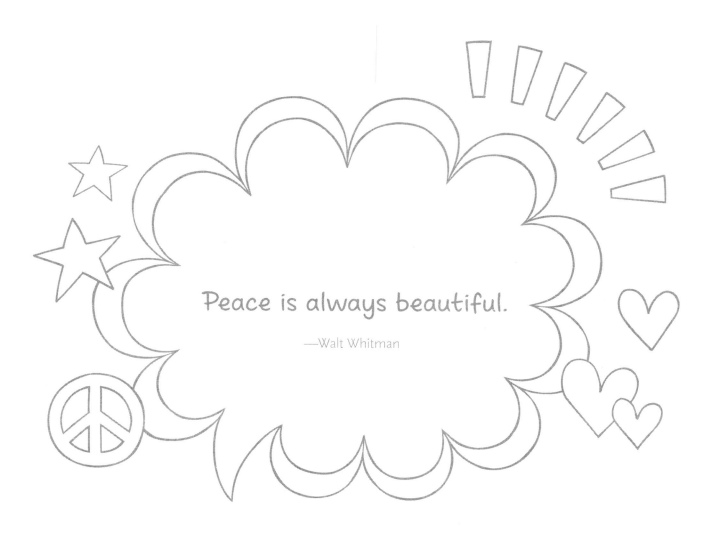

Peace is always beautiful.

—Walt Whitman

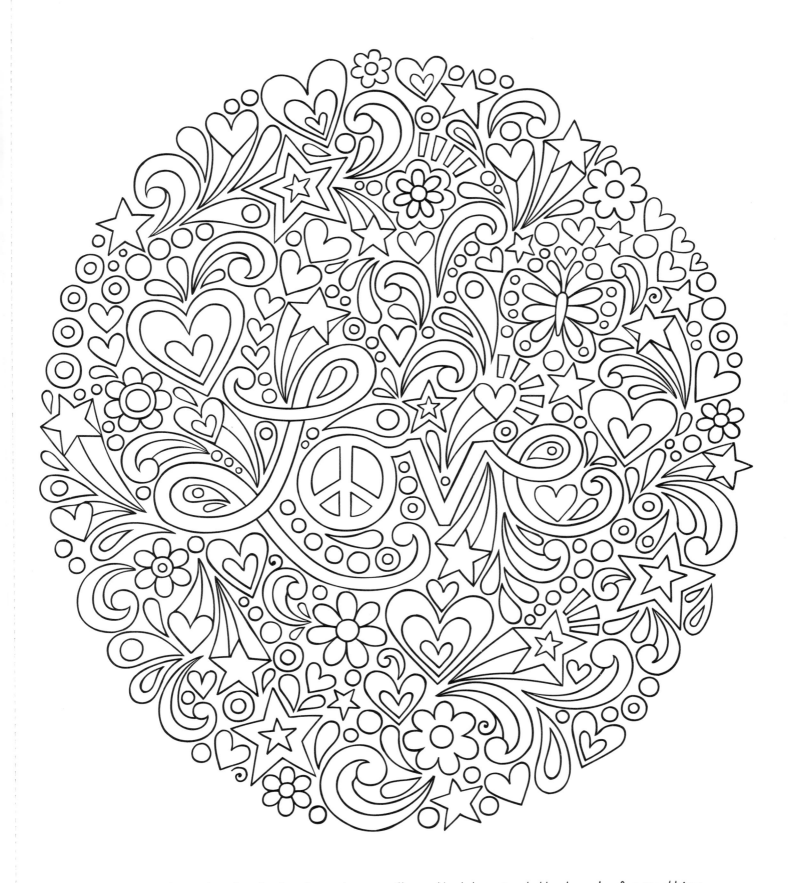

Hidden picture clue: Look closely and you will see that love is at the **heart** of everything.
(If you're puzzled, flip the page for the answer!)

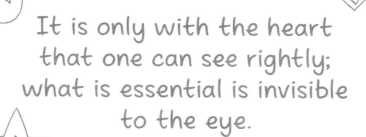

It is only with the heart
that one can see rightly;
what is essential is invisible
to the eye.

—Antoine de Saint Exupéry, *The Little Prince*

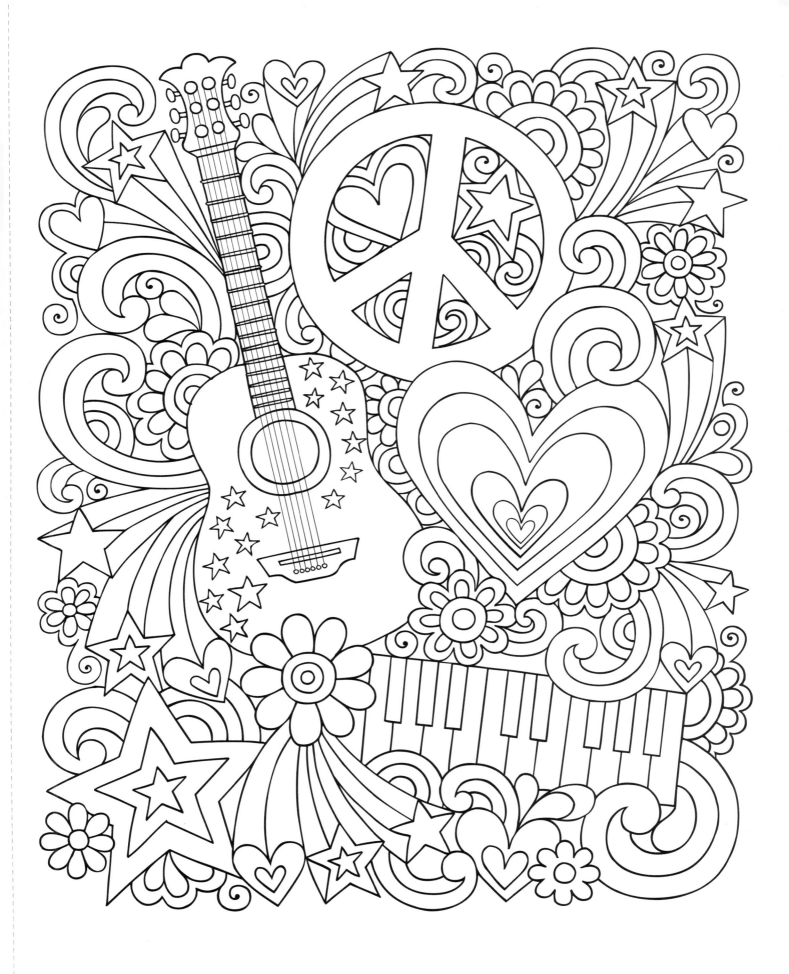

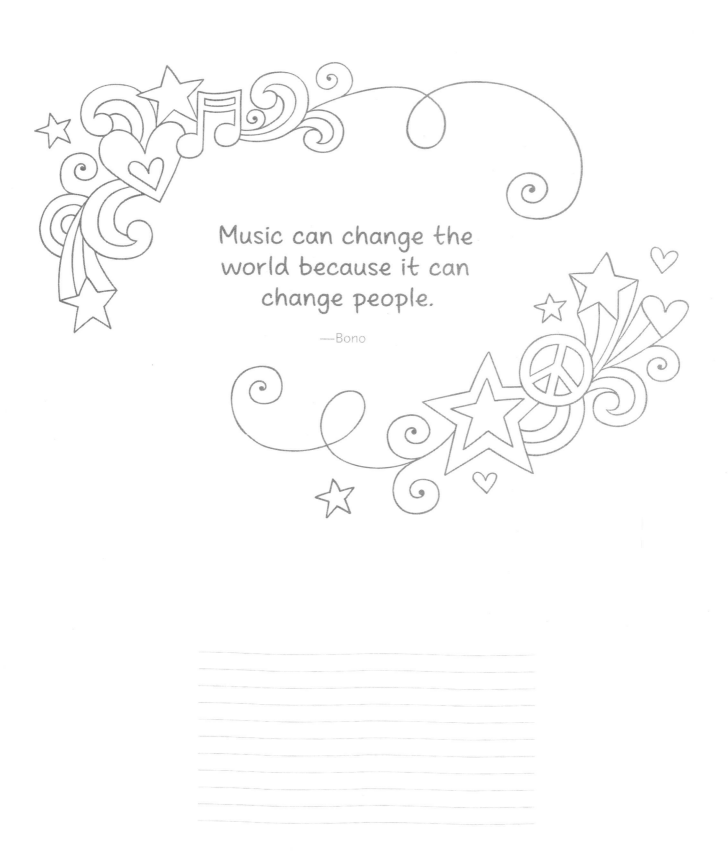

Music can change the
world because it can
change people.

—Bono

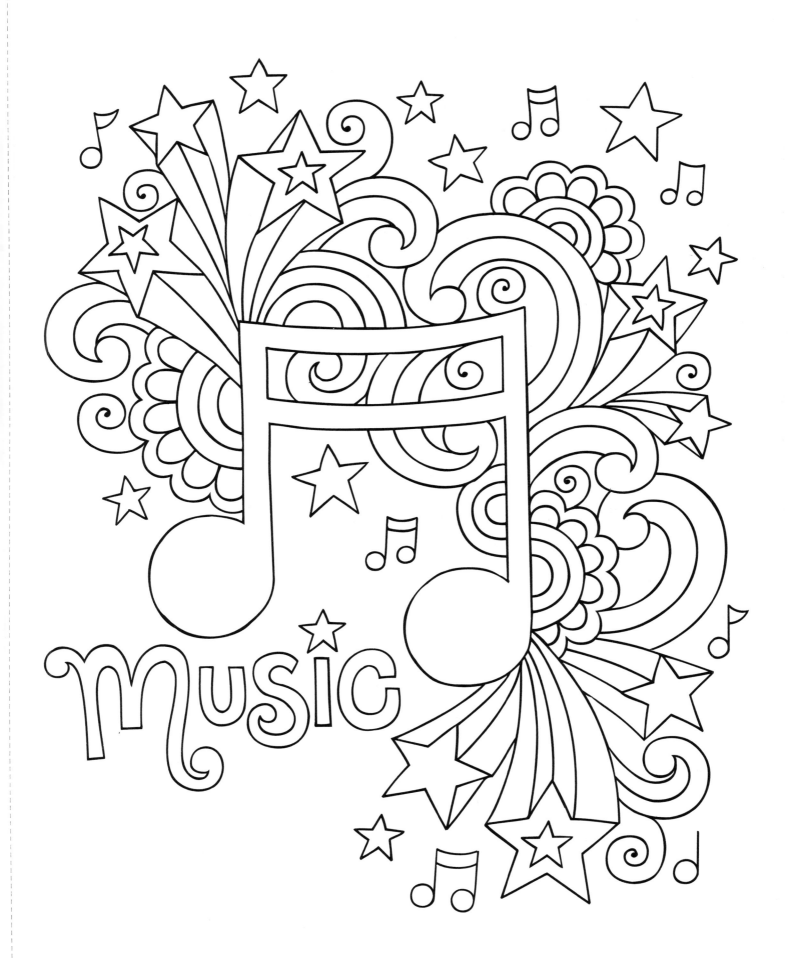

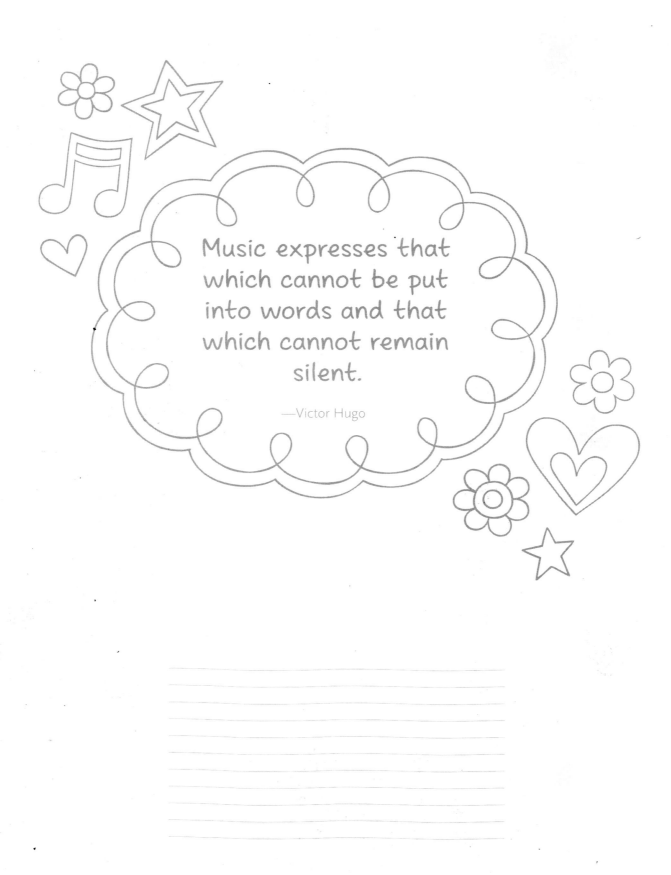

Music expresses that which cannot be put into words and that which cannot remain silent.

—Victor Hugo

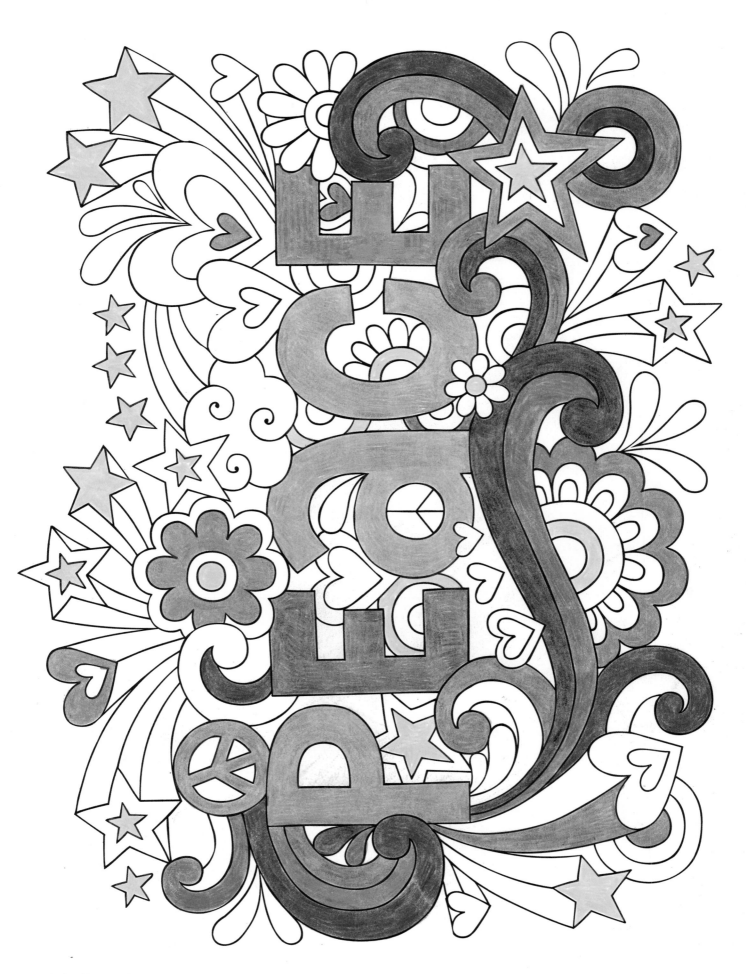

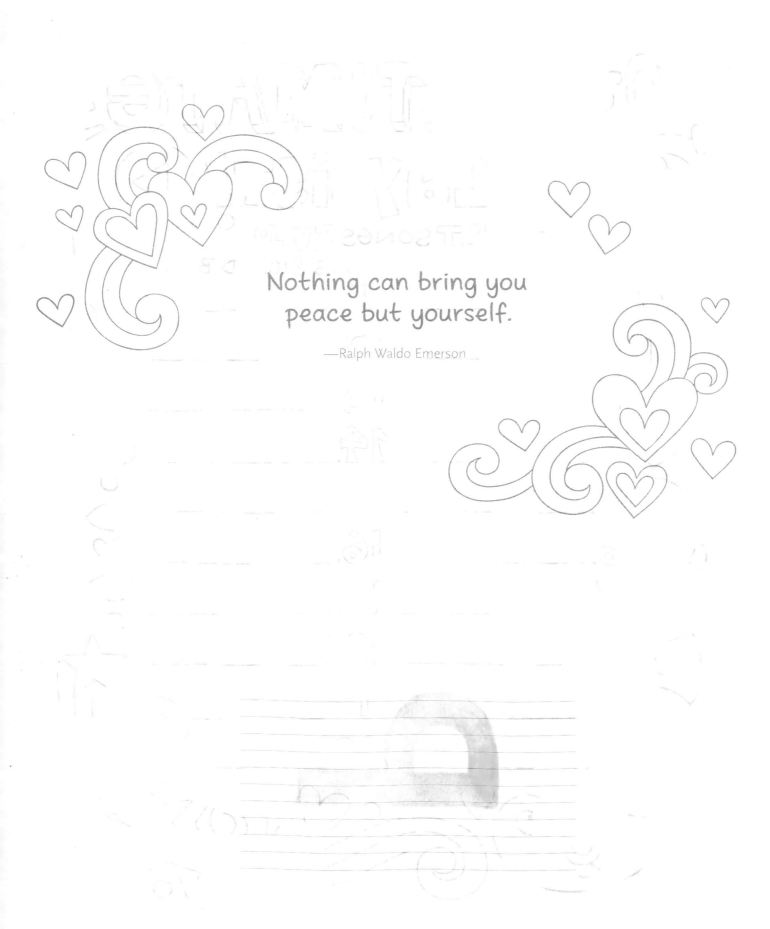

Nothing can bring you
peace but yourself.

—Ralph Waldo Emerson

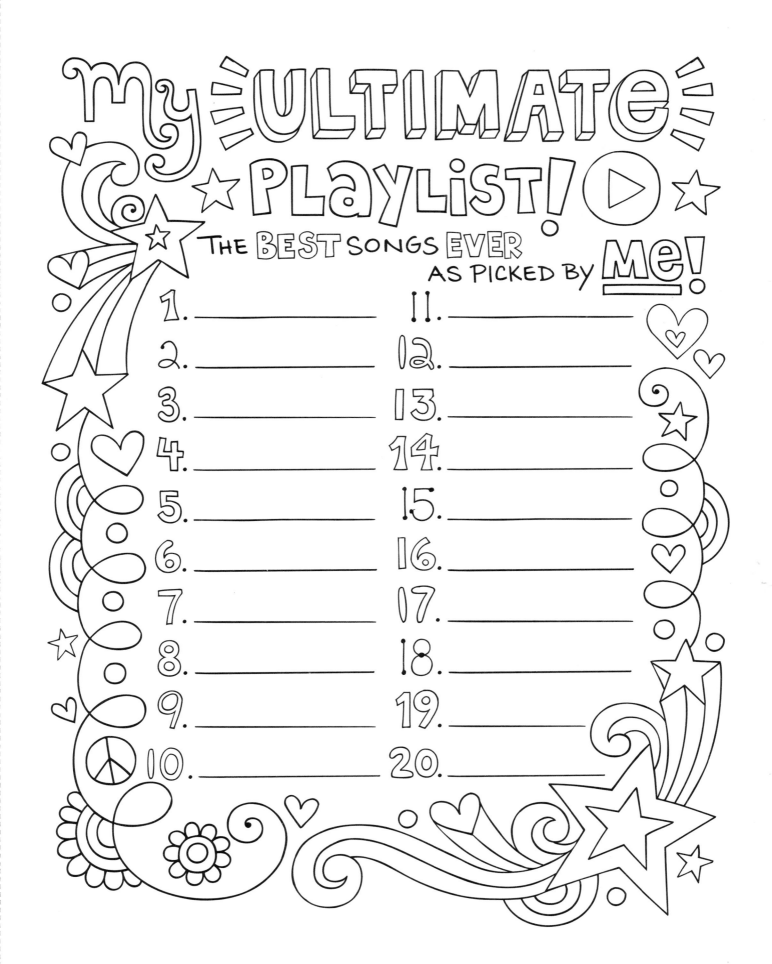

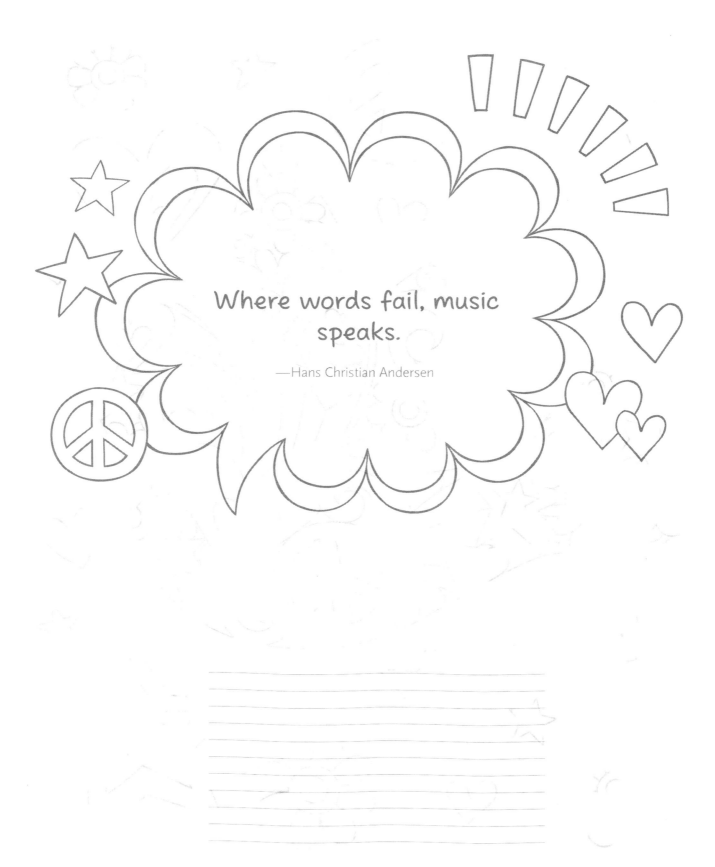

Where words fail, music speaks.

—Hans Christian Andersen

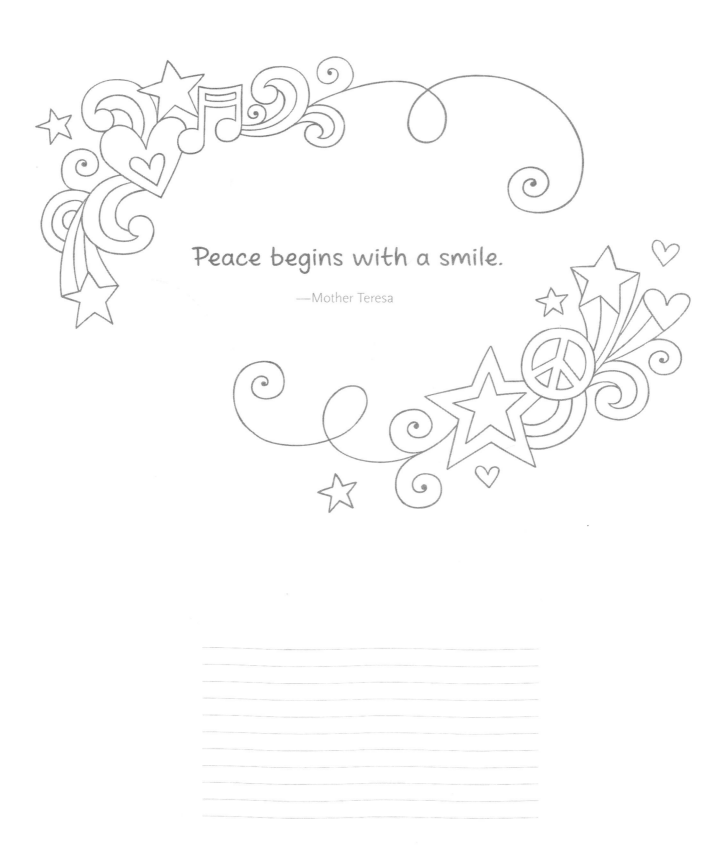

Peace begins with a smile.

—Mother Teresa

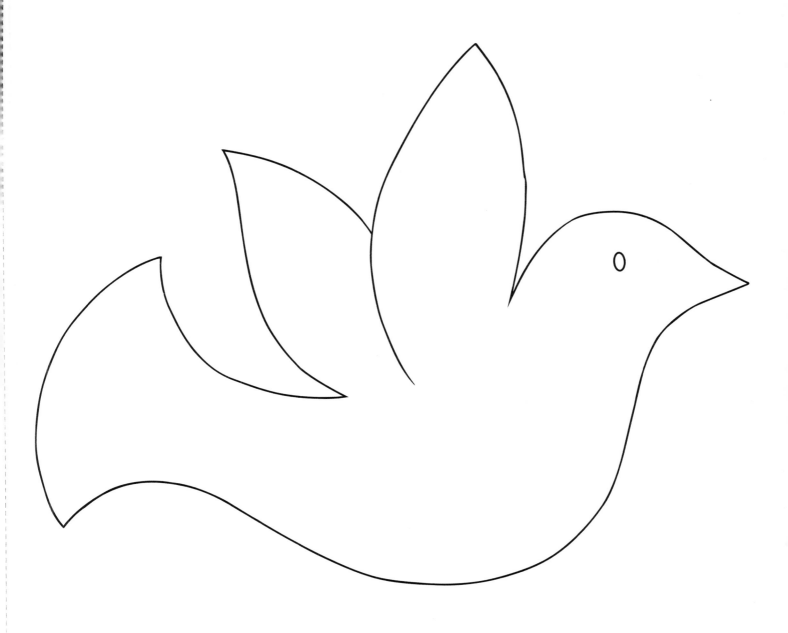

Now it's your turn! Decorate the dove with your own beautiful doodles.

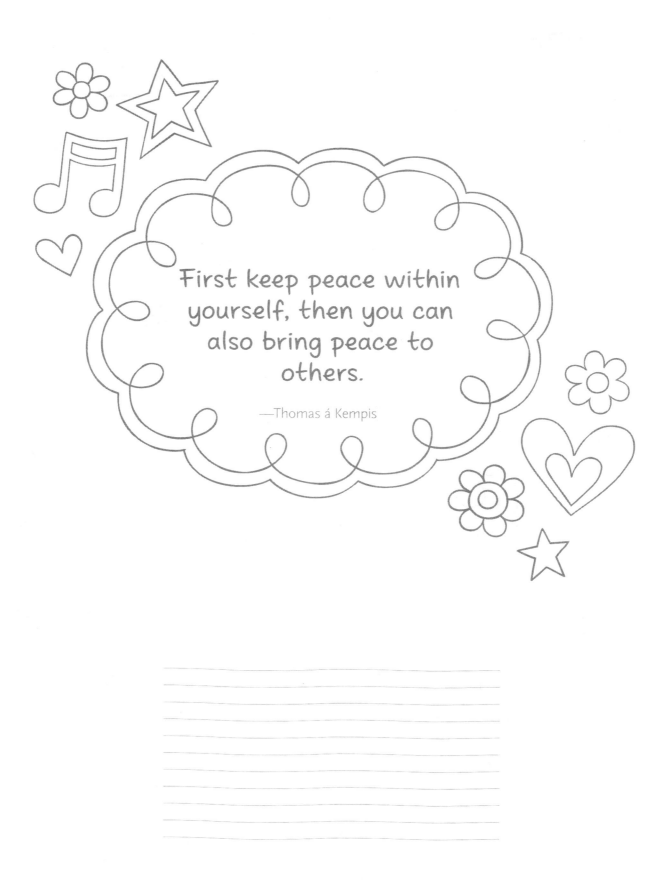

First keep peace within yourself, then you can also bring peace to others.

—Thomas á Kempis

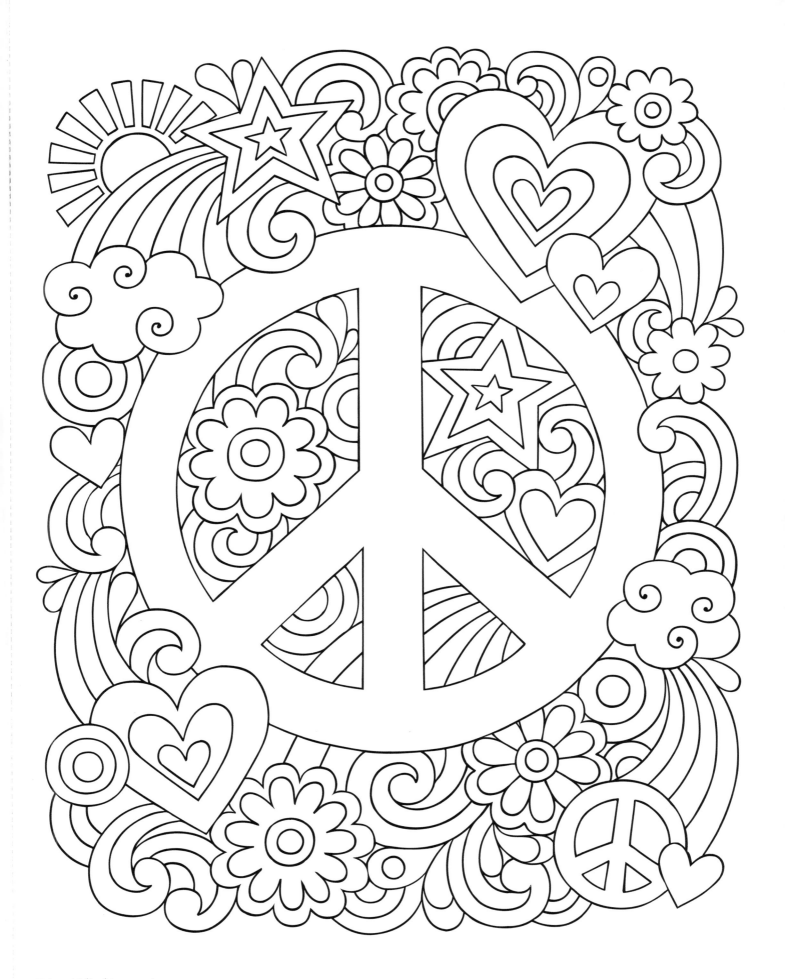

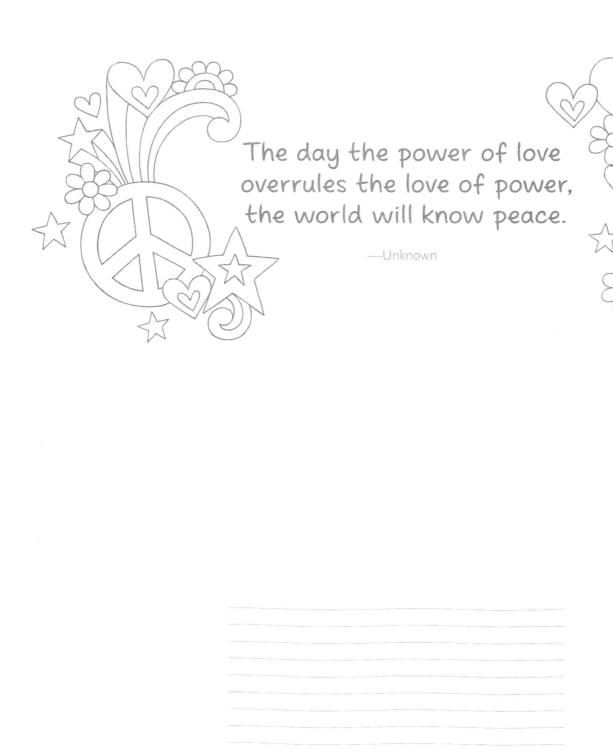

The day the power of love
overrules the love of power,
the world will know peace.

—Unknown

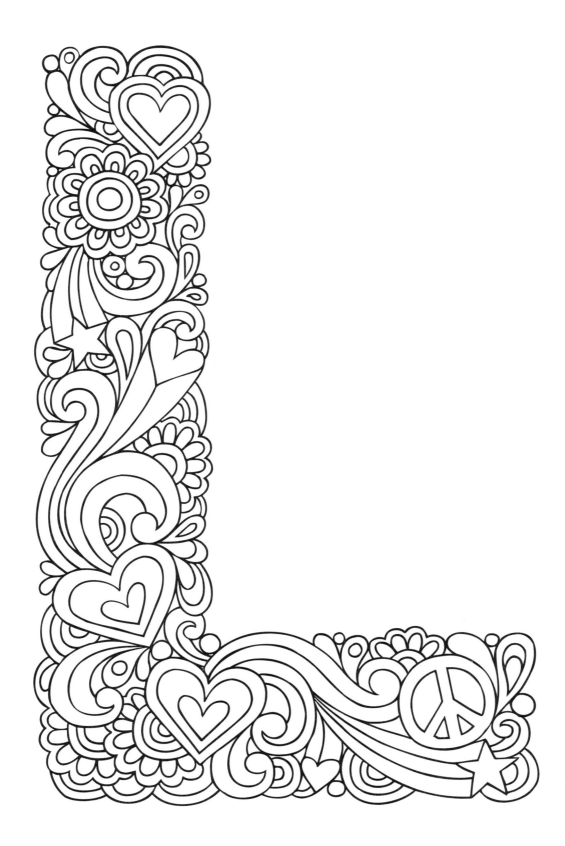

What we have once
enjoyed we can never lose.
All that we love deeply
becomes a part of us.

—Helen Keller

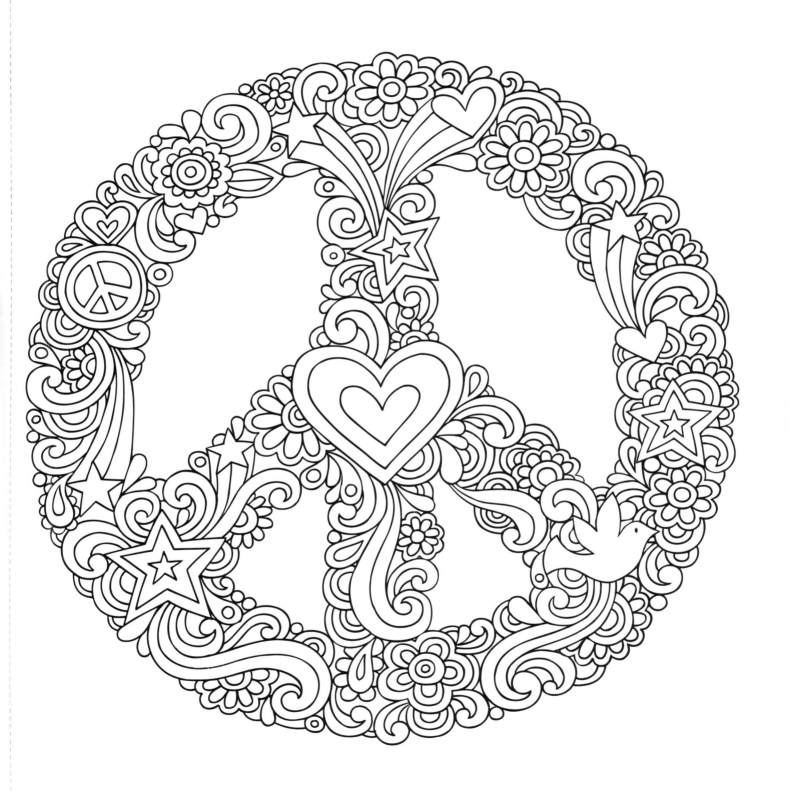

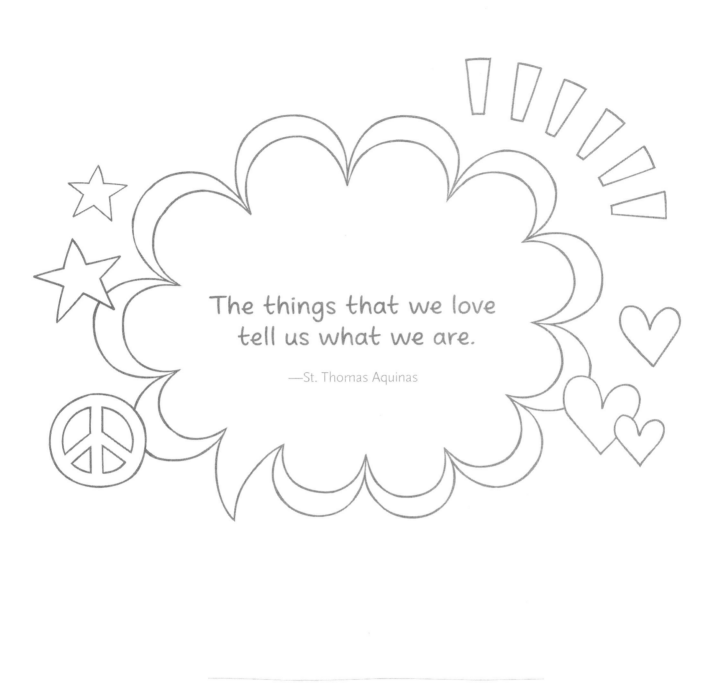

The things that we love
tell us what we are.

—St. Thomas Aquinas

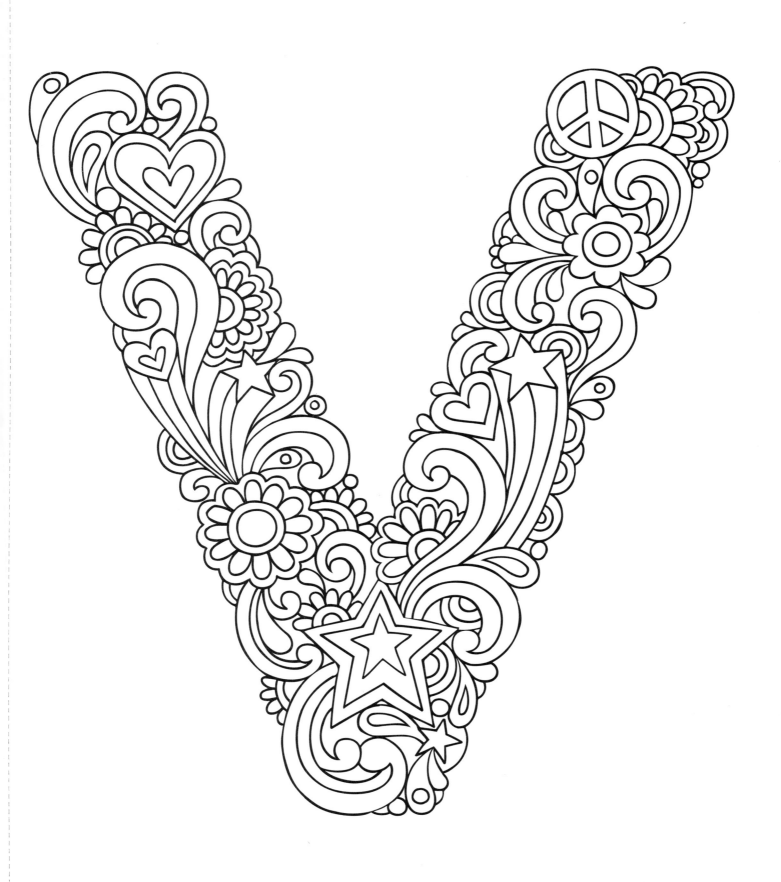

They say a person needs just three things to be truly happy in this world: someone to love, something to do, and something to hope for.

—Tom Bodett

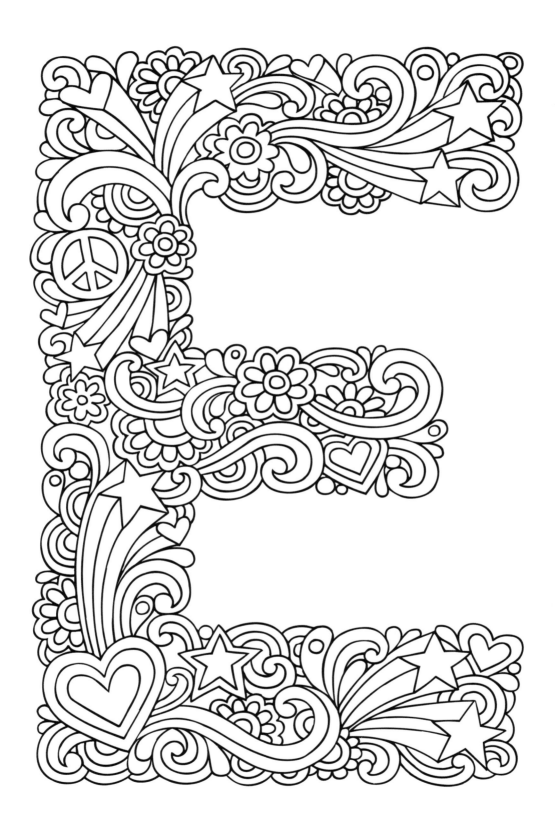

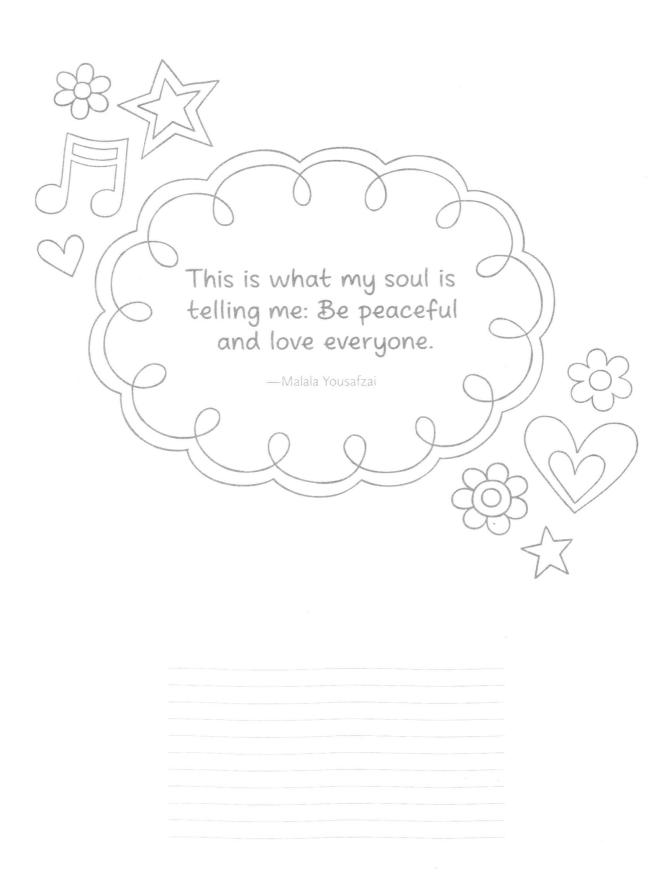

This is what my soul is telling me: Be peaceful and love everyone.

—Malala Yousafzai

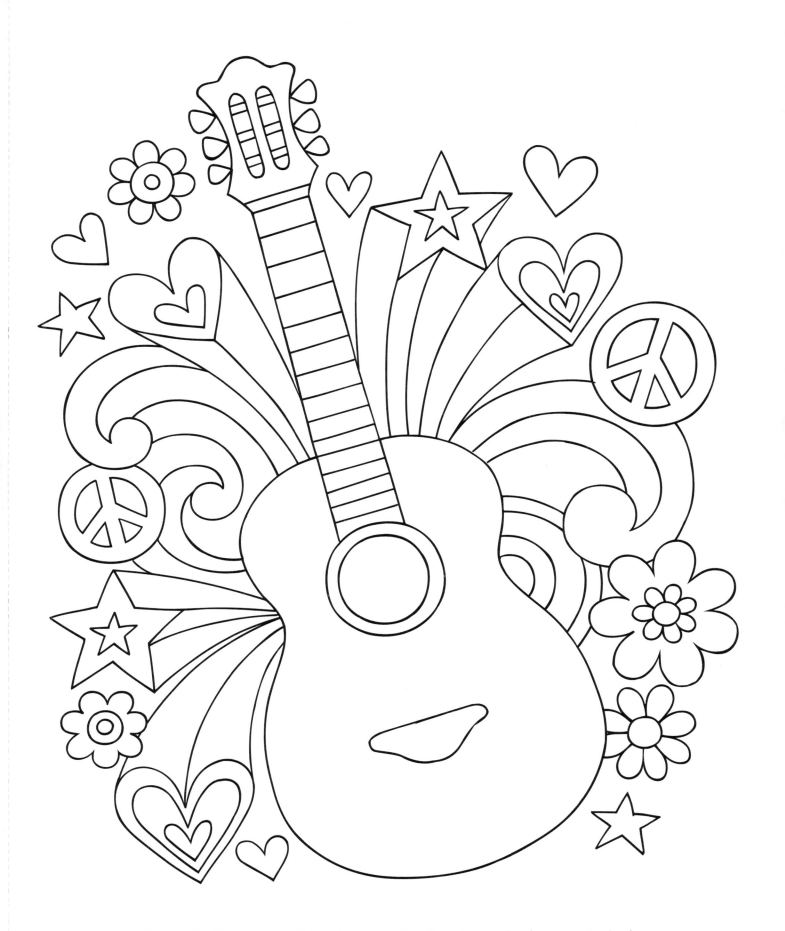

Decorate the guitar with a fabulous doodley design fit for a rock star!
Be sure to add guitar strings when you're all done.

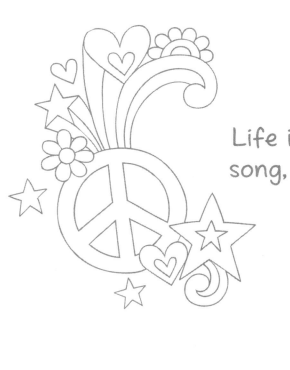

Life is one grand, sweet
song, so start the music.

—Ronald Reagan

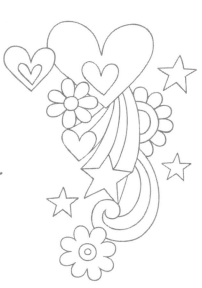

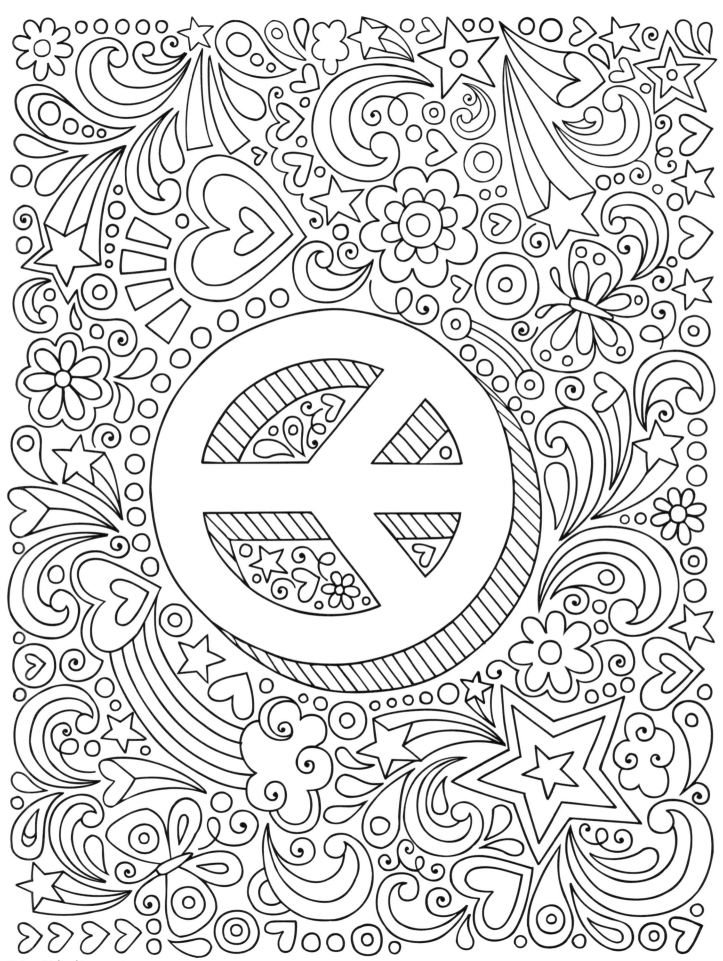

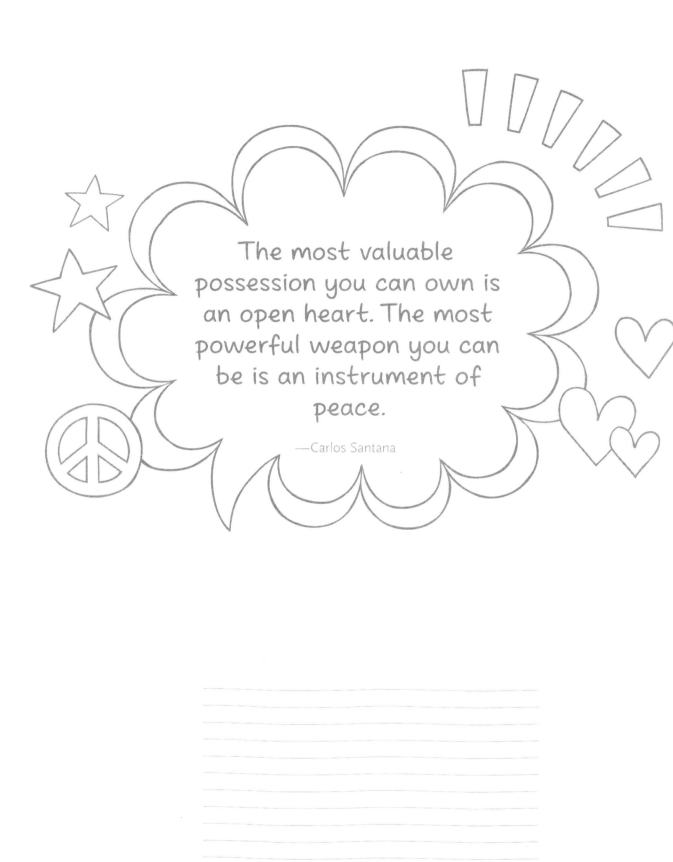

The most valuable possession you can own is an open heart. The most powerful weapon you can be is an instrument of peace.

—Carlos Santana

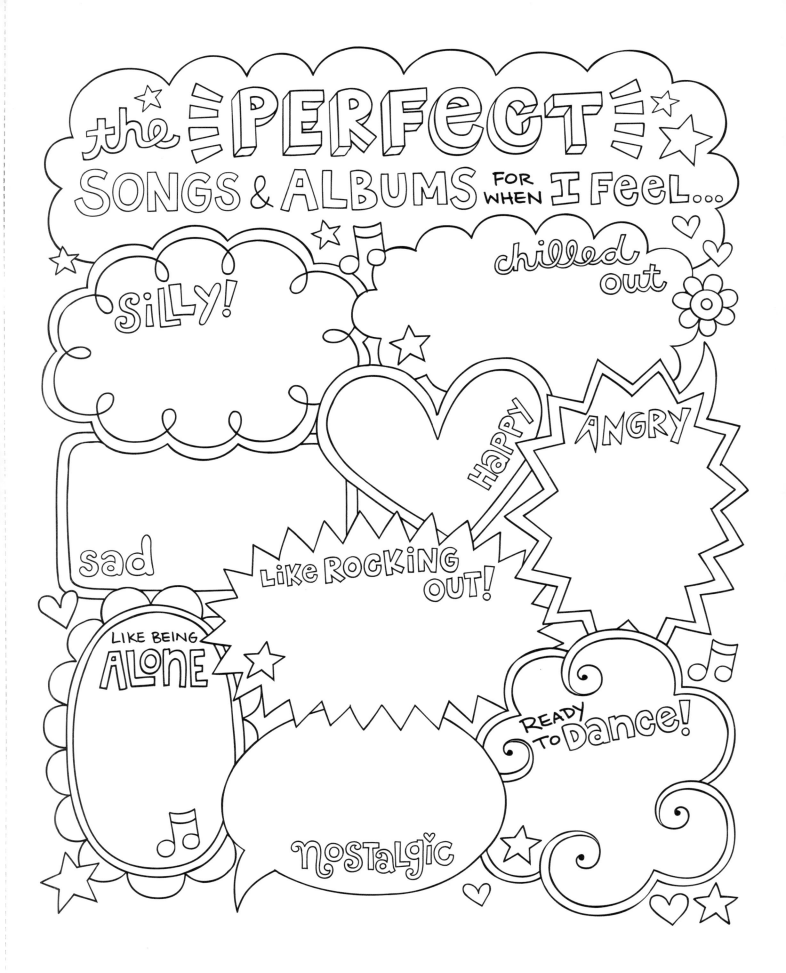

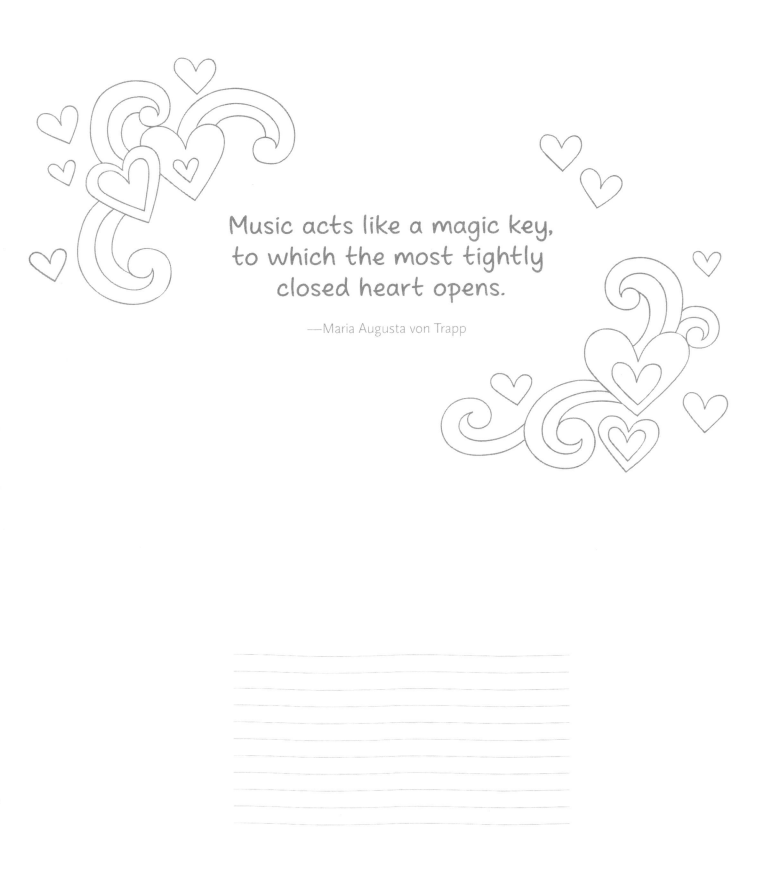

Music acts like a magic key,
to which the most tightly
closed heart opens.

—Maria Augusta von Trapp

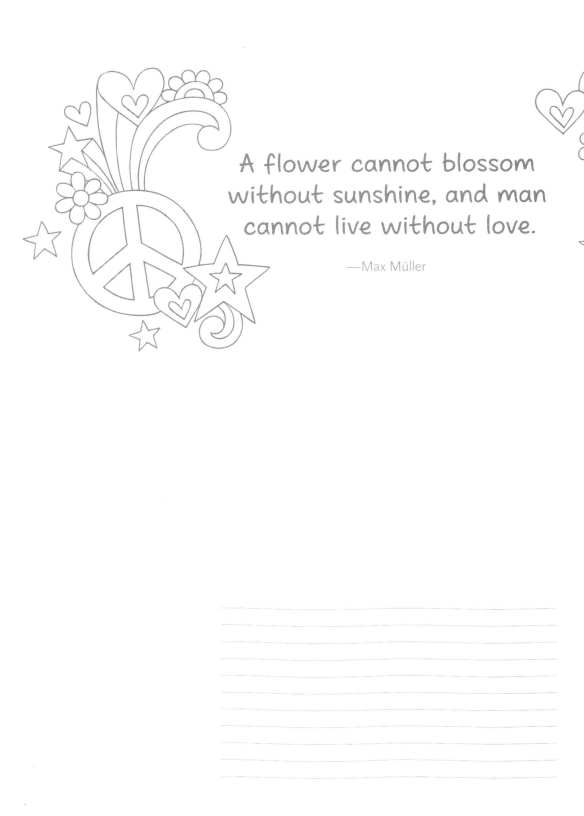

A flower cannot blossom
without sunshine, and man
cannot live without love.

—Max Müller

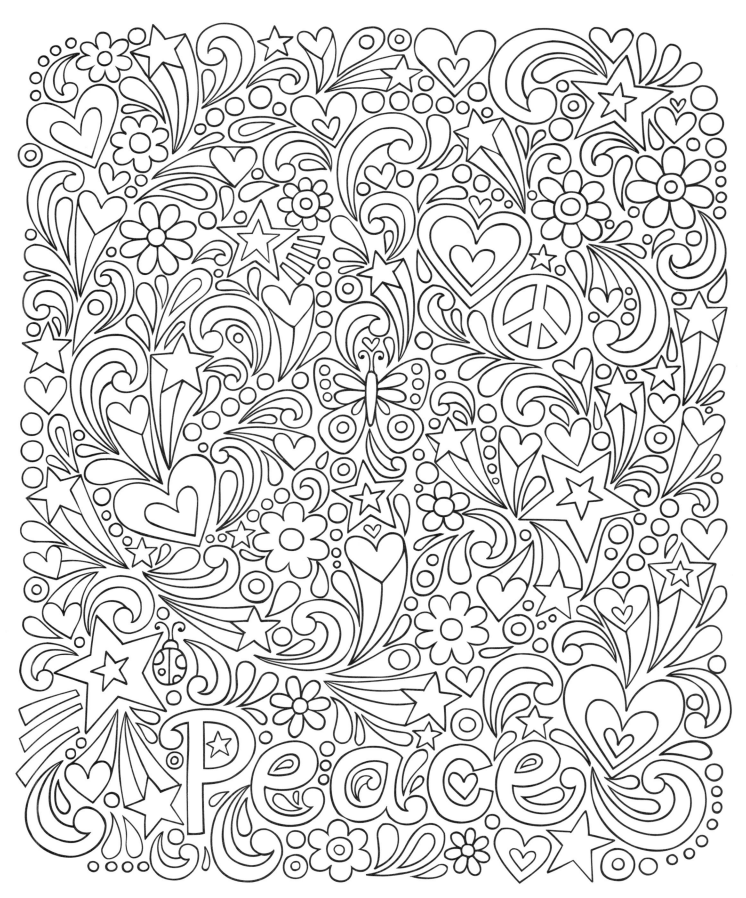

Hidden picture clue: Look closely and you will find a hidden **peace**.
(If you're puzzled, flip the page for the answer!)

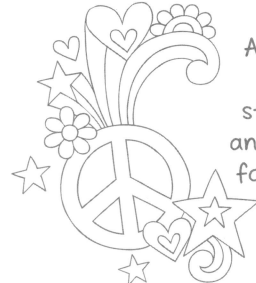

Always remember, you have within you the strength, the patience, and the passion to reach for the stars to change the world.

—Harriet Tubman

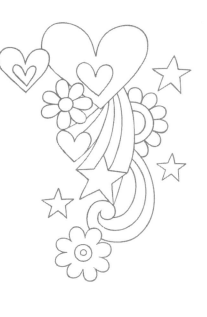

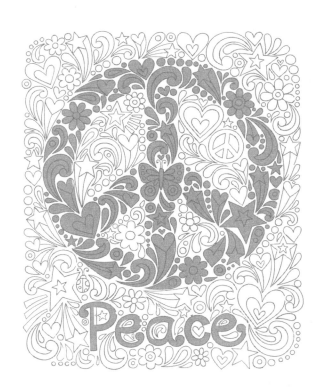

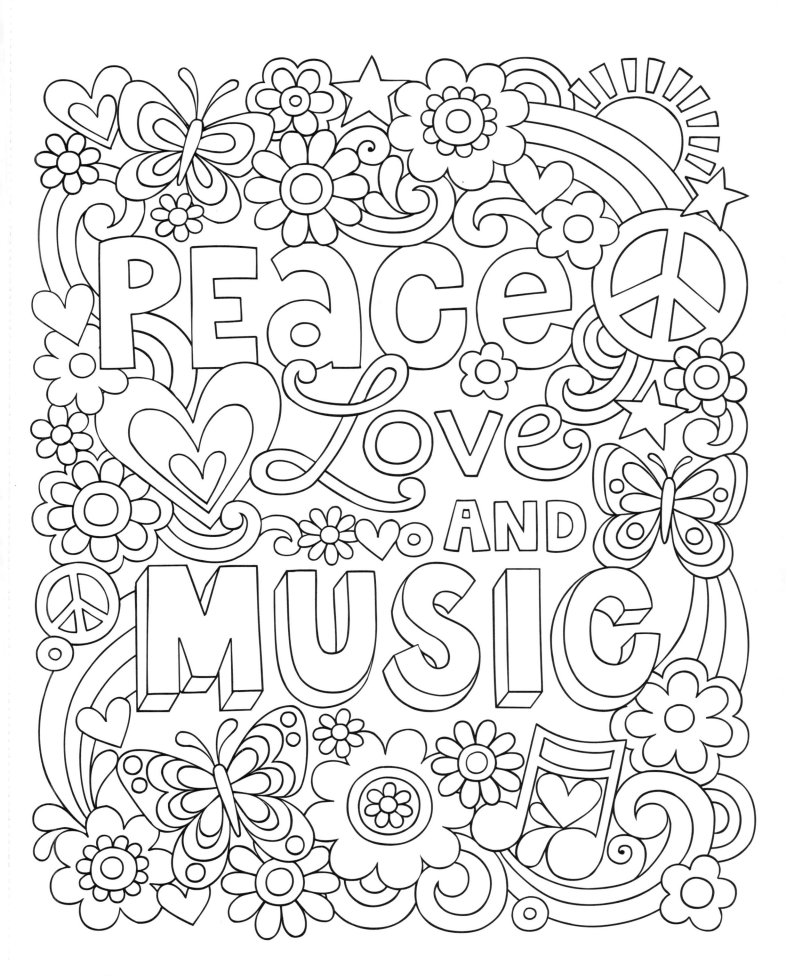

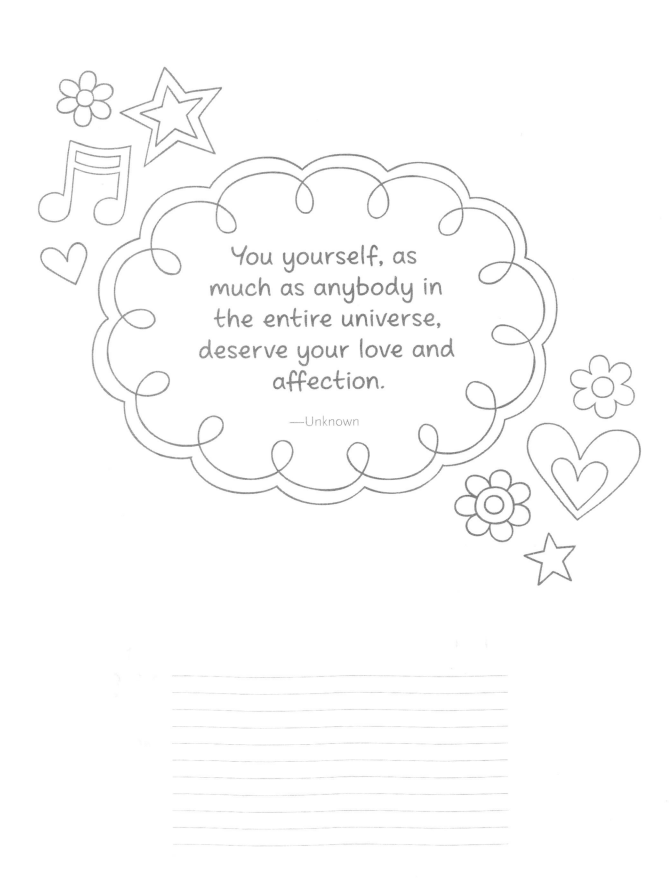

You yourself, as much as anybody in the entire universe, deserve your love and affection.

—Unknown